DEPARTMENT OF THE TREASURY
TECHNICAL EXPLANATION OF THE CONVENTION BETWEEN
THE GOVERNMENT OF THE UNITED STATES OF AMERICA AND
THE GOVERNMENT OF THE UNITED KINGDOM OF
GREAT BRITAIN AND NORTHERN IRELAND
FOR THE AVOIDANCE OF DOUBLE TAXATION AND THE PREVENTION OF FISCAL
EVASION WITH RESPECT TO TAXES ON INCOME AND ON CAPITAL GAINS

DEPARTMENT OF THE TREASURY
TECHNICAL EXPLANATION OF THE CONVENTION BETWEEN
THE GOVERNMENT OF THE UNITED STATES OF AMERICA AND
THE GOVERNMENT OF THE UNITED KINGDOM OF
GREAT BRITAIN AND NORTHERN IRELAND
FOR THE AVOIDANCE OF DOUBLE TAXATION AND THE PREVENTION OF FISCAL
EVASION WITH RESPECT TO TAXES ON INCOME AND ON CAPITAL GAINS

This is a technical explanation of the Convention between the United States and the United Kingdom of Great Britain and Northern Ireland, signed on July 24, 2001 (the "Convention"), as amended by the Protocol between the United States and the United Kingdom of Great Britain and Northern Ireland, signed on July 22, 2002 (the "Protocol"). References are made to the Convention between the Government of the United States of America and the Government of the United Kingdom of Great Britain and Northern Ireland for the Avoidance of Double Taxation and the Prevention of Fiscal Evasion with Respect to Taxes on Income and Capital Gains, signed on December 31, 1975, as amended by Protocols signed on August 26, 1976, March 31, 1977, and March 15, 1979 (the "prior Convention"). The Convention replaces the prior Convention.

In connection with the negotiation of the Convention, the delegations of the United States and the United Kingdom developed and agreed upon an exchange of diplomatic notes (the "notes"). The notes constitute an agreement between the two governments that shall enter into force at the same time as the entry into force of the Convention. These understandings and interpretations are intended to give guidance both to the taxpayers and to the tax authorities of the Contracting States in interpreting the Convention. The notes are discussed below in connection with relevant provisions of the Convention.

Negotiations took into account the U.S. Treasury Department's current tax treaty policy and the Treasury Department's Model Income Tax Convention, published on September 20, 1996 (the "U.S. Model"). Negotiations also took into account the Model Tax Convention on Income and on Capital, published by the Organization for Economic Cooperation and Development, as updated in April 2000 (the "OECD Model"), and recent tax treaties concluded by both countries.

The notes provide that the United States and the United Kingdom will consult together at regular intervals regarding the terms, operation and application of the Convention to ensure that it continues to serve the purposes of avoiding double taxation and preventing fiscal evasion. The first such consultation will take place no later than December 31st of the fifth year following the date on which the Convention enters into force in accordance with the provisions of Article 29 (Entry into Force). Further consultations shall take place thereafter at intervals of no more than five years. The notes also provide that the United States and the United Kingdom will conclude further protocols to amend the Convention, if appropriate.

The Technical Explanation is an official guide to the Convention. It reflects the policies behind particular Convention provisions, as well as understandings reached with respect to the application and interpretation of the Convention. References in the Technical Explanation to "he" or "his" should be read to mean "he or she" or "his or her."

Article 1 (General Scope)

Paragraph 1

Paragraph 1 of Article 1 provides that the Convention applies to residents of the United States or the United Kingdom, except where the terms of the Convention provide otherwise. Under Article 4 (Residence), a person is generally treated as a resident of a Contracting State if that person is, under the laws of that State, liable to tax therein by reason of his domicile, residence or other similar criteria. However, if a person is considered a resident of both Contracting States, Article 4 provides rules for determining a single State of residence (or no State of residence). This determination governs for all purposes of the Convention.

Certain provisions are applicable to persons who may not be residents of either Contracting State. For example, Article 19 (Government Service) may apply to an employee of a Contracting State who is resident in neither State. Under Article 27 (Exchange of Information and Administrative Assistance), information may be exchanged with respect to residents of third states.

Paragraph 2

Paragraph 2 states the generally accepted relationship both between the Convention and domestic law and between the Convention and other agreements between the Contracting States (*i.e.*, that no provision in the Convention may restrict any benefit accorded by the tax laws of the Contracting States, or by any other agreement between the Contracting States). The relationship between the non-discrimination provisions of the Convention and other agreements is addressed not in paragraph 2 but in paragraph 3.

Under paragraph 2, for example, if a deduction would be allowed under the U.S. Internal Revenue Code (the "Code") in computing the U.S. taxable income of a resident of the United Kingdom, the deduction also is allowed to that person in computing taxable income under the Convention. Paragraph 2 also means that the Convention may not increase the tax burden on a resident of a Contracting State beyond the burden determined under domestic law. Thus, a right to tax given by the Convention cannot be exercised unless that right also exists under internal law.

It follows that, under the principle of paragraph 2, a taxpayer's U.S. tax liability need not be determined under the Convention if the Code would produce a more favorable result. A taxpayer may not, however, choose among the provisions of the Code and the Convention in an inconsistent manner in order to minimize tax. For example, assume that a resident of the United Kingdom has three separate businesses in the United States. One is a profitable permanent establishment and the other two are trades or businesses that would earn taxable income under the Code but that do not meet the permanent establishment threshold tests of the Convention. One is profitable and the other incurs a loss. Under the Convention, the income of the permanent establishment is taxable in the United States, and both the profit and loss of the other two businesses are ignored. Under the Code, all three would be subject to tax, but the loss would offset the profits of the two profitable ventures. The taxpayer may not invoke the Convention to exclude the profit of the profitable trade or business and invoke the Code to claim the loss of the losing trade or business against the profit of the permanent establishment. *See* Rev. Rul. 84-17, 1984-1 C.B. 308. If, however, the taxpayer invokes the Code for the taxation of all three ventures, the taxpayer would not be precluded from invoking the Convention, for example, with respect to any dividend income the taxpayer may receive from the United States that is not effectively connected with any of the taxpayer's business activities in the United States.

Similarly, nothing in the Convention can be used to deny any benefit granted by any other agreement between the United States and the United Kingdom. For example, if certain benefits are provided for military personnel or military contractors under a Status of Forces Agreement between the United States and the United Kingdom, those benefits will be available to residents of the Contracting States regardless of any provisions to the contrary (or silence) in the Convention.

Paragraph 3

Paragraph 3 specifically relates to non-discrimination obligations of the Contracting States under other agreements. The provisions of paragraph 3 are an exception to the rule provided in subparagraph (b) of paragraph 2 of this article under which the Convention shall not restrict in any manner any benefit now or hereafter accorded by any other agreement between the Contracting States.

Clause (i) of subparagraph (a) of paragraph 3 provides that, notwithstanding any other agreement to which the Contracting States may be parties, a dispute concerning the interpretation or application of the Convention, including a dispute concerning whether a taxation measure is within the scope of the Convention, shall be considered only by the competent authorities of the Contracting States, and the procedures under Article 26 (Mutual Agreement Procedure) of the Convention exclusively shall apply to the dispute. Thus, dispute-resolution procedures that may be incorporated into trade, investment, or other agreements between the Contracting States shall not apply in determining the scope of the Convention.

Clause (ii) of subparagraph (a) of paragraph 3 provides that the dispute resolution procedures set forth in Article II and Article XVII of the General Agreement on Trade in Services shall not apply to any taxation measure unless the competent authorities agree that such measure is not within the scope of the non-discrimination provisions of Article 25 (Non-Discrimination) of the Convention. Accordingly, no national treatment or most-favored-nation ("MFN") obligations undertaken by the Contracting States pursuant to the GATS shall apply to a taxation measure, unless the competent authorities otherwise agree.

The Convention does not include an additional limitation on the application of other agreements that is included in the U.S. Model. The U.S. Model provision states that national-treatment or MFN obligations undertaken by the Contracting States under agreements other than the Convention (with the exception of the General Agreement on Tariffs and Trade, as applicable to trade in goods) may not apply to a taxation measure, unless the competent authorities otherwise agree. Instead of limiting the effect of other agreements, the Contracting States analyzed existing agreements that might provide such rights. As reflected in the notes, the Contracting States believe that the only agreements in force as between the two Contracting States that may impose such national treatment or MFN obligations are: the General Agreement on Trade in Services; the General Agreement on Tariffs and Trade; the Convention to Regulate the Commerce between the Territories of the United States and of his Britannick Majesty, signed in London on July 3, 1815; and the Treaty of Amity, Commerce, and Navigation, between his Britannic Majesty and the United States of America, signed at London, November 19, 1794. The interaction between the Convention and the General Agreement on Trade in Services is discussed above. The specific language of the other three agreements makes it unlikely that they would ever apply with respect to an income tax provision. However, if there were overlap between Article 25 (Non-Discrimination) and any of these agreements, benefits would be available under both agreements. In the event of such overlap, to the extent benefits are available under one of the above three agreements, and such benefits are not available under Article 25 of the Convention, a resident of a Contracting State is entitled to the benefits provided under the overlapping agreement. Conversely, if benefits available under the Convention are not available under the overlapping agreement, a resident of a Contracting State is entitled to the benefits provided by Article 25.

The notes clarify that if it is determined that some other agreement in force at the time of the signing of the Convention includes such obligations with respect to taxation measures, the Contracting States will consult with a view to ensuring the proper interaction of the Convention and such other agreement. Such consultation may result in an amendment to the Convention if necessary. Unless and until such an amendment is made, any other such agreement would apply concurrently with the Convention.

Subparagraph (b) of paragraph 3 defines a "measure" broadly. It would include, for example, a law, regulation, rule, procedure, decision, administrative action, or any other form of governmental action or guidance.

Paragraph 4

Paragraph 4 contains the traditional saving clause found in U.S. tax treaties. The Contracting States reserve their rights, except as provided in paragraph 5, to tax their residents and citizens as provided in their internal laws, notwithstanding any provisions of the Convention to the contrary. For example, if a resident of the United Kingdom performs professional services in the United States and the income from the services is not attributable to a permanent establishment in the United States, Article 7 (Business Profits) would by its terms prevent the United States from taxing the income. If, however, the resident of the United Kingdom is also a citizen of the United States, the saving clause permits the United States to include the remuneration in the worldwide income of the citizen and subject it to tax under the normal Code rules (*i.e.*, without regard to Code section 894(a)). However, subparagraph 5(a) of this Article preserves the benefits of special foreign tax credit rules applicable to the U.S. taxation of certain U.S. income of its citizens resident in the United Kingdom. See paragraph 6 of Article 24 (Relief from Double Taxation).

For purposes of the saving clause, "residence" is determined under Article 4 (Residence). Thus, an individual who is a U.S. resident under the Internal Revenue Code but who is deemed to be a resident of the United Kingdom under the tie-breaker rules of Article 4 would be subject to U.S. tax only to the extent permitted by the Convention. For example, if an individual who is not a U.S. citizen is a resident of the United States under the Code, and is also a resident of the United Kingdom under its law, and that individual has a permanent home available to him in the United Kingdom and not in the United States, he would be treated as a resident of the United Kingdom under Article 4 and for purposes of the saving clause. The United States would not be permitted to apply its statutory rules to that person if they are inconsistent with the treaty.

However, the person would be treated as a U.S. resident for U.S. tax purposes other than determining the individual's U.S. tax liability. For example, in determining under Code section 957 whether a foreign corporation is a controlled foreign corporation, shares in that corporation held by the individual would be considered to be held by a U.S. resident. As a result, other U.S. citizens or residents might be deemed to be United States shareholders of a controlled foreign corporation subject to current inclusion of Subpart F income recognized by the corporation. See Treas. Reg. section 301.7701(b)-7(a)(3). The application of the saving clause to former citizens and long-term residents is addressed not in paragraph 4 but in paragraph 6.

Paragraph 5

Some provisions are intended to provide benefits to citizens and residents even if such benefits do not exist under internal law. Paragraph 5 sets forth certain exceptions to the saving clause that preserve these benefits for citizens and residents of the Contracting States.

Subparagraph (a) lists certain provisions of the Convention that are applicable to all citizens and residents of a Contracting State, despite the general saving clause rule of paragraph 4:
> (1) Paragraph 2 of Article 9 (Associated Enterprises) grants the right to a correlative adjustment with respect to income tax due on profits reallocated under Article 9.
> (2) Subparagraph 1(b) and paragraphs 3 and 5 of Article 17 (Pensions, Social Security, Annuities, Alimony, and Child Support) provide exemptions from source or residence State taxation for certain pension distributions, social security payments and child support.
> (3) Paragraph 1 of Article 18 (Pension Scheme) provides an exemption for certain investment income of pension schemes located in the other State, while paragraph 5 provides benefits for certain contributions by or on behalf of a U.S. citizen to certain pension schemes established in the United Kingdom.
> (4) Article 24 (Relief from Double Taxation) confirms the benefit of a credit to citizens and residents of one Contracting State for income taxes paid to the other, even if such a credit may not be available under the Code.
> (5) Article 25 (Non-Discrimination) requires one Contracting State to grant national treatment to nationals of the other Contracting State in certain circumstances. Excepting this Article from the saving clause requires, for example, that the United States give such

benefits to a national of the United Kingdom even if that person is a citizen of the United States.

(6) Article 26 (Mutual Agreement Procedure) may confer benefits on residents or nationals of the Contracting States. For example, the statute of limitations may be waived for refunds and the competent authorities are permitted to use a definition of a term that differs from the internal law definition. As with the foreign tax credit, these benefits are intended to be granted by a Contracting State to its citizens and residents.

Subparagraph (b) of paragraph 5 provides a different set of exceptions to the saving clause. The benefits referred to are all intended to be granted to temporary residents of a Contracting State (for example, in the case of the United States, holders of non-immigrant visas), but not to citizens or to persons who have acquired permanent residence in that State. If beneficiaries of these provisions travel from one of the Contracting States to the other, and remain in the other long enough to become residents under its internal law, but do not acquire permanent residence status (*i.e.*, in the U.S. context, they do not become "green card" holders) and are not citizens of that State, the host State will continue to grant these benefits even if they conflict with statutory rules. The benefits preserved by this paragraph are: the host country exemptions for the following items: government service salaries and pensions under Article 19 (Government Service); certain income of visiting students, trainees, teachers, professors, and researchers under Articles 20 (Students) and 20A (Teachers); the income of diplomatic agents and consular officers under Article 28 (Diplomatic Agents and Consular Officers); and the beneficial tax treatment of pension fund contributions under paragraph 2 of Article 18 (Pension Schemes).

Paragraph 6

Under paragraph 6, each Contracting State reserves for a period of ten years its right to tax former citizens and long-term residents whose loss of citizenship or long-term resident status had as one of its principal purposes the avoidance of tax. Thus, the saving clause in paragraph 4 applies to such persons for a period of ten years. Paragraph 6 further provides that the saving clause of paragraph 4 will not apply in the case of a former citizen or long-term resident of a Contracting State who gave up that status before February 6, 1995. This date is consistent with the February 5, 1995 effective date of the amendments to section 877 made by the Health Insurance Accountability and Portability Act of 1996, § 511, Pub. L. No. 104-191, 110 Stat. 1936, 2093 (1996).

In the case of the United States, section 877 of the Code applies to former citizens and long-term residents of the United States whose loss of citizenship or long-term resident status had as one of its principal purposes the avoidance of tax. Under section 877, the United States generally treats an individual as having a principal purpose to avoid tax if either of the following criteria exceed established thresholds: (a) the average annual net income tax of such individual for the period of 5 taxable years ending before the date of the loss of status, or (b) the net worth of such individual as of the date of the loss of status. The thresholds are adjusted annually for inflation. Section 877(c) provides certain exceptions to these presumptions of tax avoidance. The notes provide a similar set of factors that will be considered in favor of the taxpayer for purposes of determining whether one of the principal purposes of a change in status of a former citizen or long-term resident is the avoidance of tax.

In the notes, the Contracting States agree that the term "long-term resident" of a Contracting State means an individual (other than a citizen of that State) who is a lawful permanent resident of that State in at least 8 of the 15 taxable years ending with the taxable year in which the individual ceased to be a long-term resident. This test is consistent with U.S. law. Under U.S. law, moreover, an individual is not treated as a lawful permanent resident for any taxable year if such individual is treated as a resident of a foreign country under the provisions of a tax treaty between the United States and the foreign country and the individual does not waive the benefits of such treaty applicable to residents of the foreign country.

Paragraph 7

Paragraph 7 is included in the Convention because the United Kingdom continues to maintain a remittance system of taxation for individuals who are resident but not domiciled in the United Kingdom. Such persons are subject to tax in the United Kingdom on non-U.K. source income only to the extent the income or gains are remitted to the United Kingdom. Under paragraph 7, such persons are entitled to the benefits of the Convention in order to reduce or eliminate tax only to the extent that the relevant income is remitted to or received in the United Kingdom. For example, if a U.K. resident who is not domiciled in the United Kingdom maintains a brokerage account in Ireland into which is paid $100 in U.S.-source dividend income, the United States may impose withholding tax at the statutory rate of 30 percent because the dividend income will not be taxed in the United Kingdom as it has not been remitted to the United Kingdom. If the dividend income instead is paid into a brokerage account in London, the U.K. resident will be subject to tax in the United Kingdom and the United States will reduce the rate of withholding tax to 15 percent.

Paragraph 8

Paragraph 8 addresses special issues presented by fiscally transparent entities such as partnerships and certain estates and trusts. In general, paragraph 8 relates to entities that are not subject to tax at the entity level, as distinct from entities that are subject to tax, but with respect to which tax may be relieved under an integrated system. This paragraph applies to any resident of a Contracting State who is entitled to income derived through an entity that is treated as fiscally transparent under the laws of either Contracting State. Entities falling under this description in the United States include partnerships, common investment trusts under section 584 and grantor trusts. This paragraph also applies to U.S. limited liability companies ("LLCs") that are treated as partnerships for U.S. tax purposes.

Under paragraph 8, an item of income, profit or gain derived by such a fiscally transparent entity will be considered to be derived by a resident of a Contracting State if a resident is treated under the taxation laws of that State as deriving the item of income. For example, if a U.K. company pays interest to an entity that is treated as fiscally transparent for U.S. tax purposes, the interest will be considered derived by a resident of the U.S. only to the extent that the taxation laws of the United States treats one or more U.S. residents (whose status as U.S. residents is determined, for this purpose, under U.S. tax law) as deriving the interest for U.S. tax purposes. In the case of a partnership, the persons who are, under U.S. tax laws, treated as partners of the entity would normally be the persons whom the U.S. tax laws would treat as deriving the interest income through the partnership. Also, it follows that persons whom the United States treats as partners but who are not U.S. residents for U.S. tax purposes may not claim a benefit for the interest paid to the entity under the Convention, because they are not residents of the United States for purposes of claiming this treaty benefit. (If, however, the country in which they are treated as resident for tax purposes, as determined under the laws of that country, has an income tax convention with the United Kingdom, they may be entitled to claim a benefit under that convention.) In contrast, if, for example, an entity is organized under U.S. laws and is classified as a corporation for U.S. tax purposes, interest paid by a U.K. company to the U.S. entity will be considered derived by a resident of the United States since the U.S. corporation is treated under U.S. taxation laws as a resident of the United States and as deriving the income.

The same result obtains even if the entity were viewed differently under the tax laws of the United Kingdom (*e.g.*, as not fiscally transparent in the first example above where the entity is treated as a partnership for U.S. tax purposes). Similarly, the characterization of the entity in a third country is also irrelevant, even if the entity is organized in that third country. The results follow regardless of whether the entity is disregarded as a separate entity under the laws of one jurisdiction but not the other, such as a single owner entity that is viewed as a branch for U.S. tax purposes and as a corporation for U.K. tax purposes. These results also obtain regardless of where the entity is organized (*i.e.*, in the United States, in the United Kingdom, or, as noted above, in a third country).

For example, income from U.S. sources received by an entity organized under the laws of the United States, which is treated for U.K. tax purposes as a corporation and is owned by a U.K. shareholder who is a U.K. resident for U.K. tax purposes, is not considered derived by the shareholder of that corporation even if, under the tax laws of the United States, the entity is treated as fiscally transparent. Rather, for purposes of the treaty, the income is treated as derived by the U.S. entity.

These principles also apply to trusts to the extent that they are fiscally transparent in either Contracting State. For example, if X, a resident of the United Kingdom, creates a revocable trust in the United States and names persons resident in a third country as the beneficiaries of the trust, X would be treated under U.S. law as the beneficial owner of income derived from the United States. In that case, the trust's income would be regarded as being derived by a resident of the United Kingdom only to the extent that the laws of the United Kingdom treat X as deriving the income for U.K. tax purposes by application of the U.K. "settlor trust" rules.

Paragraph 8 is not an exception to the saving clause of paragraph 4. Accordingly, the notes confirm that paragraph 8 does not prevent a Contracting State from taxing an entity that is treated as a resident of that State under its tax law. For example, if a U.S. LLC with U.K. members elects to be taxed as a corporation for U.S. tax purposes, the United States will tax that LLC on its worldwide income on a net basis, without regard to whether the United Kingdom views the LLC as fiscally transparent. The portion of the notes relating to Article 24 (Relief from Double Taxation) provides rules for determining which Contracting State has the primary right to tax and which State must provide a credit in such circumstances.

Article 2 (Taxes Covered)

This article specifies the U.S. and U.K. taxes to which the Convention applies.

Paragraph 1

This article identifies the taxes to which the Convention applies. Paragraph 1 is based upon the OECD Model and defines the scope of application of the Convention. The Convention applies to taxes on income and capital gains imposed on behalf of a Contracting State, irrespective of the manner in which they are levied. Except with respect to Article 25 (Non-Discrimination), state and local taxes are not covered by the Convention.

Paragraph 2

Paragraph 2 also is based upon the OECD Model and provides a definition of taxes on income and on capital gains. The Convention covers taxes on total income or any part of income and includes tax on gains derived from the alienation of property. The Convention does not apply, however, to payroll taxes. Nor does it apply to property taxes, except with respect to Article 25 (Non-Discrimination).

Paragraph 3

Paragraph 3 lists the taxes in force at the time of signature of the Convention to which the Convention applies.

Subparagraph 3(a) provides that the existing U.S. covered taxes are the Federal income taxes imposed by the Code, together with the excise taxes imposed with respect to insurance premiums paid to foreign insurers (Code sections 4371 through 4374) and with respect to private foundations (Code sections 4940 through 4948). Although the Convention continues the coverage of the insurance excise tax provided by the prior Convention, paragraph 5 of Article 7 restricts the availability of benefits under the Convention in the case of insurance policies entered into as part of a conduit arrangement. Social security taxes (Code sections 1401, 3101, 3111 and 3301) are specifically excluded from coverage, even though they may be regarded as income taxes.

In the Convention, unlike the prior Convention, the accumulated earnings tax and the personal holding company tax are covered taxes because they are income taxes and they are not otherwise excluded from coverage. Under the Code, these taxes will not apply to most foreign corporations because of a statutory exclusion or the corporation's failure to meet a statutory requirement.

The existing covered taxes of the United Kingdom are identified in subparagraph (b) of paragraph 3. In the case of the United Kingdom, the Convention applies to the income tax, the capital gains tax, the corporation tax, and the petroleum revenue tax. Paragraph 3 of Article 24 (Relief from Double Taxation), however, limits the amount of the petroleum revenue tax allowable as a credit against United States tax.

Paragraph 4

Paragraph 4 provides that the Convention will apply to any taxes that are substantially similar to those enumerated in paragraph 3, and which are imposed in addition to, or in place of, the existing taxes after July 24, 2001, the date of signature of the Convention. Paragraph 4 also provides that the U.S. and U.K. competent authorities will notify each other of any changes that have been made in their laws, both tax laws and non-tax laws, that affect significantly their obligations under the Convention. Other laws that may affect a Contracting State's obligations under the Convention may include, for example, laws affecting bank secrecy.

Article 3 (General Definitions)

Paragraph 1

Paragraph 1 defines a number of basic terms used in the Convention. Certain others are defined in other articles of the Convention. For example, the term "resident of a Contracting State" is defined in Article 4 (Residence). The term "permanent establishment" is defined in Article 5 (Permanent Establishment). The terms "dividends," "interest" and "royalties" are defined in Articles 10, 11 and 12, respectively.

The introduction to paragraph 1 makes clear that the definitions in Article 3 apply for all purposes of the Convention, unless the context requires otherwise. This latter condition allows flexibility in the interpretation of the treaty in order to avoid unintended results. Terms that are not defined in the Convention are dealt with in paragraph 2.

Subparagraph (a) defines the term "person" to include an individual, an estate, a trust, a partnership, a company and any other body of persons. The definition is significant for a variety of reasons. For example, under Article 4, only a "person" can be a "resident" and therefore eligible for most benefits under the treaty. Also, all "persons" are eligible to claim relief under Article 26 (Mutual Agreement Procedure).

The term "company" is defined in subparagraph (b) as a body corporate or an entity treated as a body corporate for tax purposes. Although the Convention does not add "in the state in which it is organized," as does the U.S. Model, the result should be same as under the U.S. Model because the Commentaries to the OECD Model interpret language identical to that of the Convention in a manner consistent with the U.S. Model.

Subparagraph (c) defines the term "enterprise" as any activity or set of activities that constitutes a trade or business. Subparagraph (d) provides that the term "business" includes the performance of professional services and other activities of an independent character. Both definitions are identical to definitions recently added to the OECD Model in connection with the deletion of Article 14 (Independent Personal Services) from the OECD Model. The inclusion of the two definitions is intended to clarify that the performance of professional services or other activities of an independent character are considered to constitute an enterprise. Accordingly, income from such activities is dealt with under Article 7 (Business Profits) and not Article 22 (Other Income). The definitions are not included in the U.S. Model because the U.S. Model continues to include a separate article regarding the treatment of independent personal services.

The terms "enterprise of a Contracting State" and "enterprise of the other Contracting State" are defined in subparagraph (e) as an enterprise carried on by a resident of a Contracting State and an enterprise carried on by a resident of the other Contracting State. An enterprise of a Contracting State need not be carried on in that State. It may be carried on in the other Contracting State or a third state (*e.g.*, a U.S. corporation doing all of its business in the United Kingdom would still be a U.S. enterprise).

Subparagraph (f) defines the term "international traffic." The term means any transport by a ship or aircraft except when the ship or aircraft is operated solely between places within the other Contracting State. This definition is applicable principally in the context of Article 8 (Shipping and Air Transport). The definition combines with paragraphs 2 and 3 of Article 8 to exempt from tax by the source State income from the rental of ships or aircraft by lessors that are operators of ships and aircraft and from the rental of containers by container leasing companies.

The exclusion from the definition of international traffic of transport by a ship or aircraft solely between places within a Contracting State means, for example, that carriage of goods or passengers solely between New York and Chicago would not be treated as international traffic, whether carried by a U.S. or a foreign carrier. The substantive taxing rules of the Convention relating to the taxation of income from transport, principally Article 8, therefore, would not apply to income from such carriage. Thus, if the carrier engaged in internal U.S. traffic were a resident of the United Kingdom (assuming that were possible under U.S. law), the United States would not be required to exempt the income from that transport under Article 8. The income would, however, be treated as business profits under Article 7 (Business Profits), and therefore would be taxable in the United States only if attributable to a U.S. permanent establishment of the foreign carrier, and then only on a net basis. The gross basis U.S. tax imposed by section 887 would never apply under the circumstances described.

If, however, goods or passengers are carried by a carrier resident in the United Kingdom from a non-U.S. port to, for example, New York, and some of the goods or passengers continue on to Chicago, the entire transport would be international traffic. The notes confirm that this would be true even if the international carrier transferred the goods at the U.S. port of entry from a ship to a land vehicle, from a ship to a lighter, or even if the overland portion of the trip in the United States was handled by an independent carrier under contract with the original international carrier, so long as both parts of the trip were reflected in original bills of lading. Thus, the result is the same as under the U.S. Model, even though the definition of "international traffic" follows the OECD Model by focusing on the ship or aircraft rather than on the transport itself.

Finally, a "cruise to nowhere" (*i.e.*, a cruise beginning and ending in a port in the same Contracting State with no stops in a foreign port) would not constitute international traffic.

Subparagraph (g) defines the term "competent authority" for the United States and the United Kingdom respectively. The U.S. competent authority is the Secretary of the Treasury or his delegate. The Secretary of the Treasury has delegated the competent authority function to the Commissioner of Internal Revenue, who in turn has delegated the authority to the Director, International (LMSB). With respect to interpretative issues, the Director acts with the concurrence of the Associate Chief Counsel (International) of the Internal Revenue Service. The U.K. competent authority is the Commissioners of Inland Revenue or their authorized representative.

The term "United States" is defined in subparagraph (h) to mean the United States of America, including the states, the District of Columbia and the territorial sea of the United States. The term does not include Puerto Rico, the Virgin Islands, Guam or any other U.S. possession or territory. The geographical meaning of the term United States also includes the territorial sea of the United States, and for certain purposes, the definition is extended to include the sea bed and subsoil of undersea areas adjacent to the territorial sea of the United States. This extension applies to the extent that the United States exercises sovereignty in accordance with international law for the purpose of natural resource exploration and exploitation of such areas. This extension of the definition applies, however, only if the person, property or activity to which the Convention is being applied is connected with such natural resource exploration or exploitation. Thus, it would not include any activity involving the sea floor of an area over which the United States exercised sovereignty for natural resource purposes if that activity was unrelated to the exploration and exploitation of natural resources.

The term "United Kingdom" is defined in subparagraph (i) to mean Great Britain and Northern Ireland, including the area of the continental shelf which has or may be designated by the United Kingdom, in accordance with international law, as an area within which the rights of the United Kingdom relating to the seabed and the subsoil and their natural resources may be exercised. The Convention does not apply to the Channel Islands or the Isle of Man.

The term "national," as it relates to the United States and to the United Kingdom, is defined in clauses (i) and (ii) of subparagraph (j). This term is relevant for purposes of Articles 19 (Government Service) and 25 (Non-discrimination). With respect to the United States, a national is (1) an individual who is a citizen of the United States, and (2) any legal person, partnership or association deriving its status as such from the law in force in the United States. With respect to the United Kingdom, a national is (1) any British citizen, (2) any British subject not possessing the citizenship of any other Commonwealth country or territory, provided he has the right of abode in the United Kingdom; and (3) any legal person, partnership, association or other entity deriving its status as such from the law in force in the United Kingdom.

The definition of the term "qualified governmental entity" in subparagraph (k) is relevant for purposes of Articles 4 (Residence) and 23 (Limitation on Benefits). The term means: (1) a Contracting State or a political subdivision or local authority of the Contracting State; and (2) a person wholly owned by a Contracting State, political subdivision or local authority of the

Contracting State, provided and such person satisfies certain organizational and funding standards and does not carry on a business. Unlike the U.S. Model, the definition of "qualified governmental entity" in subparagraph (k) does not include government pension funds, since a number of the benefits that are relevant only to government pension funds in the U.S. Model are available to all qualified pension funds in the Convention.

Subparagraph (l) states that the term "Contracting State" means the United States or the United Kingdom, as the context requires.

Subparagraph (m) defines the term "real property," which replaces the term "immovable property" in the Prior Convention. This term is relevant for purposes of Article 6 (Income from Real Property), Article 10 (Dividends), and Article 13 (Gains). Consistent with Treas. Reg. § 1.897-1(b), the term "real property" generally includes land and the unsevered products of the land, improvements, and personal property associated with the use of real property. The term does not include an interest in land solely as a creditor (*e.g.*, a mortgage interest). "Real property" specifically includes livestock and equipment used in agriculture and forestry, rights to which the provisions of general law respecting landed property apply, usufruct of real property and rights to variable or fixed payments as consideration for the working of, or the right to work, mineral deposits and other natural resources. Ships, boats and aircraft, however, are not regarded as real property.

The term "conduit arrangement" is defined in subparagraph (n). The term is used in paragraph 5 of Article 7 (Business Profits), paragraph 9 of Article 10 (Dividends), paragraph 7 of Article 11 (Interest), paragraph 5 of Article 12 (Royalties), and paragraph 4 of Article 22 (Other Income). Those rules generally apply if a resident of a Contracting State receives an item of income which qualifies for benefits under the Convention, and then that resident pays all, or substantially all, of that income to a resident of a third state who would not be entitled to equivalent (or more favorable) benefits with respect to that item of income. The rules will apply, however, only if one of the main purposes of the transaction is to increase the benefits under the Convention beyond what the ultimate recipient would have received if he had received the payment directly.

The term is not used in the OECD or U.S. Model, but is included here at the request of the United Kingdom in order to ensure that each of the Contracting States can prevent residents of third countries from improperly obtaining the benefits of the Convention. For the United Kingdom, these transaction-based anti-abuse rules are a necessary supplement to the entity-based anti-treaty shopping rules in Article 23 (Limitation on Benefits). On the other hand, U.S. domestic law provides specific anti-conduit rules (Code section 7701(l) and regulation section 1.881-3, which apply to multiple-party financing transactions), as well as a number of other domestic anti-abuse principles (such as the business purpose doctrine) that apply in the treaty context.

The United States intends to interpret the conduit arrangement provisions of the Convention in accordance with U.S. domestic law, as it may evolve over time. This intention to interpret the provisions in accordance with U.S. domestic law, as well as the United Kingdom's agreement thereto, was confirmed by the exchange of letters attached hereto as "Appendix A."

Therefore, the inclusion of these rules in the Convention does not constitute an expansion (or contraction) of U.S. domestic anti-abuse principles (except with respect to the application of anti-conduit principles to the insurance excise tax, as discussed below under paragraph 5 of Article 7). The United States intends that the inclusion of these rules only with respect to the listed articles shall create no negative inference regarding the application of U.S. domestic anti-abuse rules (*e.g.*, the anti-conduit rules and other anti-abuse rules referred to above) to those articles, other articles of the Convention, or other U.S. tax treaties. The exchange of letters referred to above provides examples of how the United States and the United Kingdom intend to apply the anti-conduit provisions of the Convention.

Subparagraph (o) defines the term "pension scheme" to include any plan, scheme, fund, trust or other arrangement established in a Contracting State which is generally exempt from income taxation in that State and which is operated principally to provide pension or retirement benefits or to earn income for the benefit of one or more such arrangements. The notes provide an agreed list of existing plans qualifying as "pension schemes" in each Contracting States. In the case of the United States, the term "pension scheme" includes the following: qualified plans under section 401(a), individual retirement plans (including individual retirement plans that are part of a simplified employee pension plan that satisfies section 408(k), individual retirement accounts, individual retirement annuities, section 408(p) accounts, and Roth IRAs under section 408A), section 403(a) qualified annuity plans, and section 403(b) plans. 401(k) plans qualify as pension schemes because a 401(k) plan is a type of 401(a) plan. In the case of the United Kingdom, the term "pension scheme" includes the following: employment-related arrangements (other than a social security scheme) approved as retirement benefit schemes for the purposes of Chapter I of Part XIV of the Income and Corporation Taxes Act 1988, and personal pension schemes approved under Chapter IV of Part XIV of that Act. The reference to entities that are operated principally to earn income for the benefit of one or more such arrangements is intended to ensure that income earned by group trusts, which invest the assets of pension schemes but do not administer pension benefits, will nevertheless qualify for benefits. The term "pension scheme" also includes any scheme identical or substantially similar to the foregoing schemes that are established pursuant to legislation introduced after the date of signature of the Convention.

Paragraph 2

Paragraph 2 provides that in the application of the Convention, any term used but not defined in the Convention will have the meaning that it has under the law of the Contracting State whose tax is being applied, unless the context requires otherwise. The paragraph makes clear that if the term is defined under both the tax and non-tax laws of a Contracting State, the definition in the tax law will take precedence over the definition in the non-tax laws. Finally, there also may be cases where the tax laws of a State contain multiple definitions of the same term. In such a case, the definition used for purposes of the particular provision at issue, if any, should be used.

If the meaning of a term cannot be readily determined under the law of a Contracting State, or if there is a conflict in meaning under the laws of the two States that creates difficulties in the application of the Convention, the competent authorities, as indicated in paragraph 3(f) of Article 25 (Mutual Agreement Procedure), may establish a common meaning in order to prevent double taxation or to further any other purpose of the Convention. This common meaning need not conform to the meaning of the term under the laws of either Contracting State.

The reference in paragraph 2 to the internal law of a Contracting State means the law in effect at the time the treaty is being applied, not the law as in effect at the time the treaty was signed. The use of "ambulatory" definitions, however, may lead to results that are at variance with the intentions of the negotiators and of the Contracting States when the treaty was negotiated and ratified. The reference in both paragraphs 1 and 2 to the "context otherwise requir[ing]" a definition different from the treaty definition, in paragraph 1, or from the internal law definition of the Contracting State whose tax is being imposed, under paragraph 2, refers to a circumstance where the result intended by the Contracting States is different from the result that would obtain under either the paragraph 1 definition or the statutory definition. Thus, flexibility in defining terms is necessary and permitted.

Article 4 (Residence)

This Article sets forth rules for determining whether a person is a resident of a Contracting State for purposes of the Convention. As a general matter only residents of the Contracting States may claim the benefits of the Convention. The treaty definition of residence is to be used only for purposes of the Convention. The fact that a person is determined to be a resident of a Contracting State under Article 4 does not necessarily entitle that person to the benefits of the Convention. In addition to being a resident, a person also must qualify for benefits under Article 23 (Limitation on Benefits) in order to receive benefits conferred on residents of a Contracting State.

The determination of residence for treaty purposes looks first to a person's liability to tax as a resident under the respective taxation laws of the Contracting States. As a general matter, a person who, under those laws, is a resident of one Contracting State and not of the other need look no further. For purposes of the Convention, that person is a resident of the State in which he is resident under internal law. If, however, a person is resident in both Contracting States under their respective taxation laws, the Article proceeds, where possible, to use tie-breaker rules to assign a single State of residence to such a person for purposes of the Convention.

The treatment of fiscally transparent entities is addressed in paragraph 8 of Article 1 of the Convention, not in Article 4 as in the U.S. Model. This placement was considered more appropriate because the rules concerning fiscally transparent entities are substantive rules of general application, not simply a definition of residence.

Paragraph 1

The term "resident of a Contracting State" is defined in paragraph 1. In general, this definition incorporates the definitions of residence in U.S. and U.K. law by referring to a resident as a person who, under the laws of a Contracting State, is subject to tax there by reason of his domicile, residence, citizenship, place of management, place of incorporation or any other similar criterion. Thus, residents of the United States include aliens who are considered U.S.

residents under Code section 7701(b). Paragraphs 2 and 3 address special cases that may arise in the context of Article 4.

Certain entities that are nominally subject to tax but that in practice are rarely required to pay tax also would generally be treated as residents and therefore accorded treaty benefits. For example, RICs, REITs and REMICs are all residents of the United States for purposes of the treaty. Although the income earned by these entities normally is not subject to U.S. tax in the hands of the entity, they are taxable to the extent that they do not currently distribute their profits, and therefore may be regarded as "liable to tax." They also must satisfy a number of requirements under the Code in order to be entitled to special tax treatment.

A person who is liable to tax in a Contracting State only in respect of income from sources within that State or capital situated therein or of profits attributable to a permanent establishment in that State will not be treated as a resident of that Contracting State for purposes of the Convention. Thus, a consular official of the United Kingdom who is posted in the United States, who may be subject to U.S. tax on U.S. source investment income, but is not taxable in the United States on non-U.S. source income, would not be considered a resident of the United States for purposes of the Convention. (See Code section 7701(b)(5)(B)). Similarly, an enterprise of the United Kingdom with a permanent establishment in the United States is not, by virtue of that permanent establishment, a resident of the United States. The enterprise generally is subject to U.S. tax only with respect to its income that is attributable to the U.S. permanent establishment, not with respect to its worldwide income, as it would be if it were a U.S. resident.

Paragraph 2

Paragraph 2 contains an exception to the general rule of paragraph 1 that residence under internal law also determines residence under the Convention. The exception applies with respect to a U.S. citizen or alien lawfully admitted for permanent residence (*i.e.*, a "green card" holder). Under paragraph 1, a person is considered a resident of a Contracting State for purposes of the Convention if he is liable to tax in that Contracting State by reason of citizenship. Although this rule applies to both Contracting States, only the United States taxes its non-resident citizens in the same manner as its residents. In addition, aliens admitted to the United States for permanent residence ("green card" holders) qualify as U.S. residents under the first sentence of paragraph 1 because they are taxed by the United States as residents, regardless of where they physically reside.

Under the exception of paragraph 2, a U.S. citizen or green card holder will be treated as a resident of the United States for purposes of the Convention, and, thereby entitled to treaty benefits, only if he meets two conditions. First, he must have a substantial presence (see section 7701(b)(3)), permanent home or habitual abode in the United States. This rule requires that the U.S. citizen or green card holder have a reasonably strong economic nexus with the United States. Second, he must not be treated as a resident of a state other than the United Kingdom under any treaty between the United Kingdom and a third state. This rule prevents a U.S. citizen or green card holder who is a resident of a country other than the United States or the United Kingdom from choosing the benefits of the Convention over those provided by the treaty between the United Kingdom and his country of residence. If the U.S. citizen or green card holder's country of residence does not have a treaty with the United Kingdom, however, then he will be treated as a resident of the United States as long as he meets the first requirement of an economic nexus. If such a person is a resident of both the United States and the United Kingdom, whether or not he is to be treated as a resident of the United States for purposes of the Convention is determined by the tie-breaker rules of paragraph 4.

Thus, for example, an individual resident of Mexico who is a U.S. citizen by birth, or who is a Mexican citizen and holds a U.S. green card, but who, in either case, has never lived in the United States, would not be entitled to benefits under the Convention. However, a U.S. citizen who is transferred to Mexico for two years would be entitled to benefits under the Convention if he maintains a permanent home or habitual abode in the United States and is not a resident of Mexico for purposes of the U.K.-Mexico tax treaty. If he were treated as a resident of Mexico under the U.K.-Mexico tax treaty, he could claim only the benefits of that treaty, even if the Convention would provide greater benefits.

The fact that a U.S. citizen who does not have close ties to the United States may not be treated as a U.S. resident under the Convention does not alter the application of the saving clause of paragraph 4 of Article 1 (General Scope) to that citizen. For example, a U.S. citizen who pursuant to the "citizen/green card holder" rule is not considered to be a resident of the United States still is taxable on his worldwide income under the generally applicable rules of the Code.

Paragraph 3

Paragraph 3 provides that certain tax-exempt entities such as pension funds and charitable organizations will be regarded as residents of a Contracting State regardless of whether they are generally liable for income tax in the State where they are established. The inclusion of this provision is intended to clarify the generally accepted practice of treating an entity that would be liable for tax as a resident under the internal law of a State but for a specific exemption from tax (either complete or partial) as a resident of that state for purposes of paragraph 1.

Subparagraph (a) of paragraph 3 applies to pension schemes, as defined in subparagraph (o) of paragraph 1 of Article 3 (General Definitions). Subparagraph (b) applies to any plan, scheme, fund, trust, company or other arrangement established in a Contracting State that is generally exempt from taxation in that State because it is operated exclusively to administer or provide employee benefits. The reference to a general exemption is intended to reflect the fact that under U.S. law, certain organizations that generally are considered to be tax-exempt entities may be subject to certain excise taxes or to income tax on their unrelated business income. Subparagraph (c) applies to an organization that is established exclusively for religious, charitable, scientific, artistic, cultural, or educational purposes and that is a resident of a Contracting State. Thus, an exempt section 501(c) organization (such as a U.S. charity) that is generally exempt from tax under U.S. law is a resident of the United States for all purposes of the Convention. Subparagraph (d) applies to a qualified governmental entity, as defined in subparagraph (k) of paragraph 1 of Article 3, if it is the Contracting State itself, is established in a Contracting State or is a part of that State.

Paragraph 4

If, under the laws of the two Contracting States, and, thus, under paragraph 1, an individual is deemed to be a resident of both Contracting States, a series of tie-breaker rules are provided in paragraph 4 to determine a single State of residence for that individual. These tests are to be applied in the order in which they are stated. The first test is based on where the individual has a permanent home. If that test is inconclusive because the individual has a permanent home available to him in both States, he will be considered to be a resident of the Contracting State where his personal and economic relations are closest (*i.e.*, the location of his "centre of vital interests"). If that test is also inconclusive, or if he does not have a permanent home available to him in either State, he will be treated as a resident of the Contracting State where he maintains an habitual abode. If he has an habitual abode in both States or in neither of them, he will be treated as a resident of the Contracting State of which he is a national. If he is a national of both States or of neither, the matter will be considered by the competent authorities, who will assign a single State of residence.

Paragraph 5

Dual residents other than individuals (*e.g.*, companies, trusts, and estates) are addressed by paragraph 5. If such a person is, under the rules of paragraph 1, resident in both Contracting States, the competent authorities shall seek to determine a single State of residence for that person for purposes of the Convention. For example, a company is treated as resident in the United States if it is created or organized under the laws of the United States or a political subdivision. Under U.K. law, a company is treated as a resident of the United Kingdom if it is either established there or managed and controlled there. Dual residence, therefore, can arise if a U.S. company is managed and controlled in the United Kingdom. Paragraph 5 provides that the competent authorities will try to determine a single State of residence for such a company.

If the competent authorities do not reach an agreement on the single State of residence, that person may not claim any benefit provided by the Convention, except those provided by paragraph 4 of Article 24 (Relief from Double Taxation), Article 25 (Non-Discrimination), and Article 26 (Mutual Agreement Procedure). Thus, for example, a State cannot discriminate against a dual resident company, and such a company can bring issues to the competent authorities.

Dual resident companies also may be treated as resident for purposes other than that of obtaining benefits under the Convention. For example, if a dual resident company pays a dividend to a resident of the United Kingdom, the U.S. paying agent would withhold on that dividend at the appropriate treaty rate because reduced withholding is a benefit enjoyed by the resident of the United Kingdom, not by the dual resident. The dual resident company that paid the dividend would, for this purpose, be treated as a resident of the United States under the Convention. In addition, information relating to dual resident companies can be exchanged under the Convention because, by its terms, Article 27 (Exchange of Information and Administrative Assistance) is not limited to residents of the Contracting States.

Paragraph 6

Paragraph 6 carries over the rule from the prior Convention that, for U.K. tax purposes, the domicile of a woman who is a U.S. national and who was married before January 1, 1974 to a man domiciled in the United Kingdom will be determined as if such marriage took place on January 1, 1974.

As discussed above in connection with paragraph 7 of Article 1 (General Scope), the United Kingdom taxes differently the income of a U.K. resident from sources outside the United Kingdom, depending upon whether the U.K. resident is domiciled in the United Kingdom. A U.K. resident domiciled in the United Kingdom is subject to full U.K. taxation on all income, including income from sources outside the United Kingdom. A U.K. resident domiciled outside the United Kingdom, however, generally is subject to tax on income from sources outside the United Kingdom only to the extent such income is remitted to the United Kingdom.

Under U.K. law before January 1, 1974, the domicile of a woman was the same as the domicile of her husband. This rule was repealed for years beginning after December 31, 1973. As a transitional rule, however, U.K. law treats a woman married before 1974 as retaining her husband's domicile unless and until she changes her domicile by acquisition or revival of another domicile after 1973. As a consequence, under U.K. law, a female U.S. citizen who married a U.K. domiciliary male before January 1, 1974, does not have the same opportunity to prove a domicile outside the United Kingdom as does a male U.S. citizen who married a U.K. domiciliary female before January 1, 1974. Paragraph 6 of the Convention equalizes the treatment of male and female U.S. citizens in this situation.

Article 5 (Permanent Establishment)

This Article defines the term "permanent establishment," a term that is significant for several articles of the Convention. The existence of a permanent establishment in a Contracting State is necessary under Article 7 (Business Profits) for the taxation by that State of the business profits of a resident of the other Contracting State. Articles 10, 11 and 12 (dealing with dividends, interest, and royalties, respectively) provide for reduced rates of tax at source on payments of these items of income to a resident of the other State only when the income is not attributable to a permanent establishment that the recipient has in the source State. The concept is also relevant in determining which Contracting State may tax certain gains under Article 13 (Gains) and certain "other income" under Article 22 (Other Income).

The Article follows closely both the OECD Model and the U.S. Model provisions. It does not differ significantly from the definition of a permanent establishment in the prior Convention.

Paragraph 1

The basic definition of the term "permanent establishment" is contained in paragraph 1. As used in the Convention, the term means a fixed place of business through which the business of an enterprise is wholly or partly carried on. As indicated in the OECD Commentary to Article 5 (see paragraphs 4 through 8), a general principle to be observed in determining whether a permanent establishment exists is that the place of business must be "fixed" in the sense that a particular building or physical location is used by the enterprise for the conduct of its business, and that it must be foreseeable that the enterprise's use of this building or other physical location will be more than temporary.

Paragraph 2

Paragraph 2 lists a number of types of fixed places of business that constitute a permanent establishment. This list is illustrative and non-exclusive. According to paragraph 2, the term permanent establishment includes a place of management, a branch, an office, a factory, a workshop, and a mine, oil or gas well, quarry or other place of extraction of natural resources.

Paragraph 3

This paragraph provides rules to determine whether a building site or a construction or installation project constitutes a permanent establishment for the contractor, installer, etc. An activity does not create a permanent establishment unless the site, project, etc. lasts or continues for more than twelve months. This provision differs from the U.S. Model in that it does not cover offshore drilling rigs. Special rules regarding exploration and exploitation of natural resources are found in Article 21 (Offshore Exploration and Exploitation Activities).

The twelve-month test applies separately to each site or project. The twelve-month period begins when work (including preparatory work carried on by the enterprise) physically begins in a Contracting State. A series of contracts or projects by a contractor that are interdependent both commercially and geographically are to be treated as a single project for purposes of applying the twelve-month threshold test. For example, the construction of a housing development would be considered as a single project even if each house were constructed for a different purchaser.

In applying this paragraph, time spent by a sub-contractor on a building site is counted as time spent by the general contractor at the site for purposes of determining whether the general contractor has a permanent establishment. However, for the sub-contractor itself to be treated as having a permanent establishment, the sub-contractor's activities at the site must last for more than 12 months. If a sub-contractor is on a site intermittently, then, for purposes of applying the 12-month rule, time is measured from the first day the sub-contractor is on the site until the last day (*i.e.*, intervening days that the sub-contractor is not on the site are counted).

These interpretations of the Article are based on the Commentary to paragraph 3 of Article 5 of the OECD Model, which contains language that is substantially the same as that in the Convention. These interpretations are consistent with the generally accepted international interpretation of the relevant language in paragraph 3 of Article 5 of the Convention.

If the twelve-month threshold is exceeded, the site or project constitutes a permanent establishment from the first day of activity.

Paragraph 4

This paragraph contains exceptions to the general rule of paragraph 1, listing a number of activities that may be carried on through a fixed place of business, but which nevertheless do not create a permanent establishment. The use of facilities solely to store, display or deliver merchandise belonging to an enterprise does not constitute a permanent establishment of that enterprise. The maintenance of a stock of goods belonging to an enterprise solely for the purpose of storage, display or delivery, or solely for the purpose of processing by another enterprise does not give rise to a permanent establishment of the first-mentioned enterprise. The maintenance of a fixed place of business solely for the purpose of purchasing goods or merchandise, or for collecting information, for the enterprise, or for other activities that have a preparatory or auxiliary character for the enterprise, such as advertising, or the supply of information, do not constitute a permanent establishment of the enterprise. Thus, as explained in paragraph 22 of the OECD Commentary, a news bureau of a newspaper would not constitute a permanent establishment of the newspaper.

Subparagraph 4(f) provides that a combination of the activities described in the other subparagraphs of paragraph 4 will not give rise to a permanent establishment if the combination results in an overall activity that is of a preparatory or auxiliary character. This combination rule, derived from the OECD Model, differs from that in the U.S. Model. In the U.S. Model, any combination of otherwise excepted activities is not deemed to give rise to a permanent establishment, without the additional requirement that the combination, as distinct from each constituent activity, be preparatory or auxiliary. It is assumed that if preparatory or auxiliary activities are combined, the combination generally will also be of a character that is preparatory or auxiliary. If, however, this is not the case, a permanent establishment may result from a combination of such activities.

Paragraph 5

Paragraphs 5 and 6 specify when activities carried on by an agent on behalf of an enterprise create a permanent establishment of that enterprise. Under paragraph 5, a dependent agent of an enterprise is deemed to be a permanent establishment of the enterprise if the agent has and habitually exercises an authority to conclude contracts that are binding on the enterprise. If, however, the agent's activities are limited to those activities specified in paragraph 4 which would not constitute a permanent establishment if carried on by the enterprise through a fixed place of business, the agent is not a permanent establishment of the enterprise.

The OECD Model uses the term "in the name of that enterprise" rather than "binding on the enterprise." There is no substantive difference. As indicated in paragraph 32 to the OECD Commentary on Article 5, paragraph 5 of the Article is intended to encompass a person who "concludes contracts which are binding on the enterprise, even if those contracts are not actually in the name of the enterprise."

The contracts referred to in paragraph 5 are those relating to the essential business operations of the enterprise rather than ancillary activities. For example, if the agent has no authority to conclude contracts in the name of the enterprise with its customers for the sale of the goods produced by the enterprise, but it can enter into service contracts in the name of the enterprise for the enterprise's business equipment used in the agent's office, this contracting authority would not fall within the scope of the paragraph, even if exercised regularly.

Paragraph 6

Under paragraph 6, an enterprise is not deemed to have a permanent establishment in a Contracting State merely because it carries on business in that State through an independent agent, including a broker or general commission agent, if the agent is acting in the ordinary course of his business as an independent agent. Thus, there are two conditions that must be satisfied: the agent must be both legally and economically independent of the enterprise, and the agent must be acting in the ordinary course of its business in carrying out activities on behalf of the enterprise.

Whether the agent and the enterprise are independent is a factual determination. Among the questions to be considered are the extent to which the agent operates on the basis of instructions from the enterprise. An agent that is subject to detailed instructions regarding the conduct of its operations or comprehensive control by the enterprise is not legally independent.

In determining whether the agent is economically independent, a relevant factor is the extent to which the agent bears business risk. Business risk refers primarily to risk of loss. An independent agent typically bears risk of loss from its own activities. In the absence of other factors that would establish dependence, an agent that shares business risk with the enterprise, or has its own business risk, is economically independent because its business activities are not integrated with those of the principal. Conversely, an agent that bears little or no risk from the activities it performs is not economically independent and therefore is not described in paragraph 6.

Another relevant factor in determining whether an agent is economically independent is whether the agent has an exclusive or nearly exclusive relationship with the principal. Such a relationship may indicate that the principal has economic control over the agent. A number of principals acting in concert also may have economic control over an agent. The limited scope of the agent's activities and the agent's dependence on a single source of income may indicate that the agent lacks economic independence. It should be borne in mind, however, that exclusivity is not in itself a conclusive test; an agent may be economically independent notwithstanding an exclusive relationship with the principal if it has the capacity to diversify and acquire other clients without substantial modifications to its current business and without substantial harm to its business profits. Thus, exclusivity should be viewed merely as a pointer to further investigation of the relationship between the principal and the agent. Each case must be addressed on the basis of its own facts and circumstances.

Paragraph 7

This paragraph clarifies that a company that is a resident of a Contracting State is not deemed to have a permanent establishment in the other Contracting State merely because it controls, or is controlled by, a company that is a resident of that other Contracting State, or that carries on business in that other Contracting State. The determination whether a permanent establishment exists is made solely on the basis of the factors described in paragraphs 1 through 6 of the Article. Whether a company is a permanent establishment of a related company, therefore, is based solely on those factors and not on the ownership or control relationship between the companies.

Article 6 (Income from Real Property)

Paragraph 1

The first paragraph of Article 6 states the general rule that income of a resident of a Contracting State derived from real property situated in the other Contracting State may be taxed in the Contracting State in which the property is situated. Subparagraph (m) of paragraph 1 of Article 3 (General Definitions) defines the term "real property" for this purpose.

Paragraph 1 specifies that income from real property includes income from agriculture and forestry. Income from agriculture and forestry are dealt with in Article 6 rather than in Article 7 (Business Profits). Given the availability of the net basis taxation under the tax laws of each of the Contracting States, taxpayers generally should be able to obtain the same tax treatment in the State where the real property is situated regardless of whether the income is treated as business profits or income from real property.

This Article does not grant an exclusive taxing right to the situs State; the situs State is merely given the primary right to tax. The Article does not impose any limitation in terms of rate or form of tax on the situs State.

Paragraph 2

Paragraph 2 makes clear that all forms of income derived from the exploitation of real property are taxable in the Contracting State in which the property is situated. In the case of a net lease of real property, the gross rental payment (before deductible expenses incurred by the lessee) may be treated as income from the property. Income from the disposition of an interest in real property, however, is not considered "derived" from real property and is not dealt with in this article. The taxation of that income is addressed in Article 13 (Gains). Also, the interest paid on a mortgage on real property and distributions by a U.S. Real Estate Investment Trust are not dealt with in Article 6. Such payments would fall under Articles 10 (Dividends), 11 (Interest) or 13 (Gains). Finally, dividends paid by a United States Real Property Holding Corporation are not considered to be income from the exploitation of real property: such payments would fall under Article 10 (Dividends) or 13 (Gains).

Paragraph 3

This paragraph specifies that the basic rule of paragraph 1 (as elaborated in paragraph 2) applies to income from real property of an enterprise. This clarifies that the situs country may tax the real property income (including rental income) of a resident of the other Contracting State in the absence of attribution to a permanent establishment in the situs State. This provision represents an exception to the general rule under Article 7 (Business Profits) that income must be attributable to a permanent establishment in order to be taxable in the host state.

Article 7 (Business Profits)

This Article provides rules for the taxation by a Contracting State of the business profits of an enterprise of the other Contracting State.

Paragraph 1

Paragraph 1 states the general rule that business profits of an enterprise of one Contracting State may not be taxed by the other Contracting State unless the enterprise carries on business in that other Contracting State through a permanent establishment (as defined in Article 5 (Permanent Establishment)) situated there. When that condition is met, the State in which the permanent establishment is situated may tax the enterprise on the income that is attributable to the permanent establishment.

Although the Convention does not include a definition of "business profits," the term is intended to have the same meaning as under paragraph 7 of Article 7 of the U.S. Model, except that it now covers income from independent personal services because of the elimination of a separate article dealing with independent personal services, as discussed in connection with the definitions of "enterprise" and "business" in the Technical Explanation to Article 3 (General Definitions) above. Thus, the term "business profits" generally means income derived from any trade or business.

In accordance with this broad definition, the term "business profits" includes income attributable to notional principal contracts and other financial instruments to the extent that the income is attributable to a trade or business of dealing in such instruments or is otherwise related to a trade or business (as in the case of a notional principal contract entered into for the purpose of hedging currency risk arising from an active trade or business). Any other income derived from such instruments is, unless specifically covered in another article, dealt with under Article 22 (Other Income).

The term also includes income earned by an enterprise from the furnishing of personal services. Thus, a consulting firm resident in one State whose employees or partners perform services in the other State through a permanent establishment may be taxed in that other State on a net basis under Article 7, and not under Article 14 (Income from Employment), which applies only to income of employees. This change is consistent with the OECD Model, according to which income derived from professional services or other activities of an independent character is dealt with under Article 7 as business profits. With respect to the enterprise's employees themselves, however, their salary remains subject to Article 14.

Because this article applies to income earned by an enterprise from the furnishing of personal services, the article also applies to income derived by a partner resident in a Contracting State that is attributable to personal services performed in the other Contracting State through a partnership with a permanent establishment in that other State. Income which may be taxed under this article includes all income attributable to the permanent establishment in respect of the performance of the personal services carried on by the partnership (whether by the partner himself, other partners in the partnership, or by employees assisting the partners) and any income from activities ancillary to the performance of those services (*e.g.*, charges for facsimile services). Income that is not derived from the performance of personal services and that is not ancillary thereto (*e.g.*, rental income from subletting office space) is governed by other articles of the Convention.

The application of Article 7 to a service partnership may be illustrated by the following example: a partnership formed in the United Kingdom has five partners (who agree to split profits equally), four of whom are resident and perform personal services only in the United Kingdom at Office A, and one of whom performs personal services at Office B, a permanent establishment in the United States. In this case, the four partners of the partnership resident in the United Kingdom may be taxed in the United States in respect of their share of the income attributable to the permanent establishment, Office B. The services giving rise to income which may be attributed to the permanent establishment would include not only the services performed by the one resident partner, but also, for example, if one of the four other partners came to the United States and worked on an Office B matter there, the income in respect of those services. Income from the services performed by the visiting partner would be subject to tax in the United States regardless of whether the visiting partner actually visited or used Office B while performing services in the United States.

Paragraph 2

Paragraph 2 provides rules for the attribution of business profits to a permanent establishment. The Contracting States will attribute to a permanent establishment the profits that it would have earned had it been a distinct and separate enterprise engaged in the same or similar activities under the same or similar conditions and dealing wholly independently with the enterprise of which it is a permanent establishment. The "attributable to" concept of paragraph 2 is analogous but not entirely equivalent to the "effectively connected" concept in Code section 864(c). The profits attributable to a permanent establishment may be from sources within or without a Contracting State. However, as stated in paragraph 2, the business profits attributable to a permanent establishment include only those profits derived from the assets used, risks assumed, and activities performed by, the permanent establishment. This rule overrides the "residual force of attraction" rule of section 864(c)(3).

The language of paragraph 2, when combined with paragraph 3 dealing with the allowance of deductions for expenses incurred for the purposes of earning the profits, incorporates the arm's-length standard for purposes of determining the profits attributable to a permanent establishment. As noted below with respect to Article 9, the United States generally interprets the arm's length standard in a manner consistent with the OECD Transfer Pricing Guidelines.

The notes confirm that any of the methods provided by the OECD Transfer Pricing Guidelines apply, by analogy, in determining the profits attributable to a permanent establishment. Because transactions between branches of a single legal entity do not have independent legal significance, the Transfer Pricing Guidelines, which address transactions between legal entities, can apply only "by analogy".

Moreover, in applying the Transfer Pricing Guidelines, it is necessary to take into account the different economics that arise from operating through a single legal entity rather than through separate legal entities. For example, an entity that operates through branches rather than separate subsidiaries will have lower capital requirements because all of the assets of the entity are available to support all of the entity's liabilities (with some exceptions attributable to local regulatory restrictions). This is the reason that most commercial banks and some insurance companies operate through branches rather than subsidiaries. The benefit that comes from such lower capital costs must be allocated among the branches in an appropriate manner. This issue does not arise in the case of an enterprise that operates through separate entities, since each entity will have to be separately capitalized or will have to compensate another entity for providing capital (usually through a guarantee).

Under U.S. domestic regulations, internal "transactions" generally are not recognized because they do not have legal significance. In contrast, the rule provided by the notes is that such internal dealings may be used to allocate income in cases where the dealings accurately reflect the allocation of risk within the enterprise. One example is that of global trading in securities. In many cases, banks use internal swap transactions to transfer risk from one branch to a central location where traders have the expertise to manage that particular type of risk. Under the Convention, such a bank may also use such swap transactions as a means of allocating income between the branches, if use of that method is the "best method" within the meaning of regulation section 1.482-1(c). The books of a branch will not be respected, however, when the results are inconsistent with a functional analysis. So, for example, income from a transaction that is booked in a particular branch (or home office) will not be treated as attributable to that location if the sales and risk management functions that generate the income are performed in another location.

It is also permissible to use methods other than separate accounting to determine the arm's length profits of a permanent establishment when such a method would be permissible under the Transfer Pricing Guidelines. This might occur, for example, when the affairs of the permanent establishment are so closely bound up with those of the head office that it would be impossible to disentangle them on any strict basis of accounts. Because the use of profits methods is permissible under paragraph 2, it is not necessary for the Convention to include a provision corresponding to paragraph 4 of Article 7 of the OECD Model.

The Convention does not include the rule found in Paragraph 4 of the U.S. Model and paragraph 5 of Article 7 of the OECD Model. The rule provides that no business profits can be attributed to a permanent establishment merely because it purchases goods or merchandise for the enterprise of which it is a part. The rule in the both Models applies only to an office that performs functions for the enterprise in addition to purchasing. The income attribution issue does not arise if the sole activity of the permanent establishment is the purchase of goods or merchandise because such activity does not give rise to a permanent establishment under Article 5 (Permanent Establishment). A common situation in which paragraph 4 is relevant is one in which a permanent establishment purchases raw materials for the enterprise's manufacturing operation conducted outside the United States and sells the manufactured product. While business profits may be attributable to the permanent establishment with respect to its sales activities, no profits are attributable to it with respect to its purchasing activities. This result is inconsistent with the arm's length principle, since a distinct and separate enterprise would have received some compensation to perform that service. Accordingly, the rule was not included in the Convention.

Paragraph 3

This paragraph is the same as paragraph 3 of Article 7 of the OECD Model. Paragraph 3 provides that in determining the business profits of a permanent establishment, deductions shall be allowed for the expenses incurred for the purposes of the permanent establishment, ensuring that business profits will be taxed on a net basis. This rule is not limited to expenses incurred exclusively for the purposes of the permanent establishment, but includes expenses incurred for the purposes of the enterprise as a whole, or that part of the enterprise that includes the permanent establishment. Deductions are to be allowed regardless of which accounting unit of the enterprise books the expenses, so long as they are incurred for the purposes of the permanent establishment. For example, a portion of the interest expense recorded on the books of the home office in one State may be deducted by a permanent establishment in the other if properly allocable thereto. The amount of expense that must be allowed as a deduction is determined by applying the arm's length principle.

As noted above, the notes provide that the OECD Transfer Pricing Guidelines apply, by analogy, in determining the profits attributable to a permanent establishment. Accordingly, a permanent establishment may deduct payments made to its head office or another branch in compensation for services performed for the benefit of the branch. The method to be used in calculating that amount will depend on the terms of the arrangements between the branches and head office. For example, the enterprise could have a policy, expressed in writing, under which each business unit could use the services of lawyers employed by the head office. At the end of each year, the costs of employing the lawyers would be allocated to each business unit according to the amount of services used by that business unit during the year. Since this appears to be a kind of cost-sharing arrangement and the allocation of costs is based on the benefits received by each business unit, it would be an acceptable means of determining a permanent establishment's deduction for legal expenses. Alternatively, the head office could agree to employ lawyers at its own risk, and to charge an arm's length price for legal services performed for a particular business unit. If the lawyers were under-utilized, and the "fees" received from the business units were less than the cost of employing the lawyers, then the head office would bear the excess cost. If the "fees" exceeded the cost of employing the lawyers, then the head office would keep the excess to compensate it for assuming the risk of employing the lawyers. If the enterprise acted in accordance with this agreement, this method would be an acceptable alternative method for calculating a permanent establishment's deduction for legal expenses.

The notes also specify that a permanent establishment cannot be funded entirely with debt, but must have sufficient capital to carry on its activities as if it were a distinct and separate enterprise. To the extent that the permanent establishment does not have such capital, a Contracting State may attribute such capital to the permanent establishment and deny an interest deduction to the extent necessary to reflect that capital attribution. The method prescribed by U.S. domestic law for making this attribution is found in Treas. Reg. Section 1.882-5. Section 1.882-5(a)(2) states that the method is to be used in determining the amount of interest expense attributable to the business profits of a permanent establishment under U.S. tax treaties. Accordingly, a U.K. taxpayer may continue to use that method for determining its interest expense if it so chooses.

However, section 1.882-5 does not take into account the fact that some assets are more risky than other assets. An independent enterprise would need less capital to support a perfectly-hedged U.S. Treasury security than it would need to support an equity security or other asset with significant market and/or credit risk. Accordingly, in some cases section 1.882-5 would require a taxpayer to allocate more capital to the United States (and therefore would reduce the taxpayer's interest deduction) than is appropriate. To address these cases, the notes allow a taxpayer to apply a more flexible approach that takes into account the relative risk of its assets in the various jurisdictions in which it does business. In particular, in the case of financial institutions other than insurance companies, the amount of capital attributable to a permanent establishment is determined by allocating the institution's total equity between its various offices on the basis of the proportion of the financial institution's risk-weighted assets attributable to each of them. This recognizes the fact that financial institutions are in many cases required to risk-weight their assets for regulatory purposes and, in other cases, will do so for business reasons even if not required to do so by regulators. However, the taxpayer is not required to apply this treaty method for determining its interest deduction. As noted above, it may choose to apply the rule of Treas. Reg. Section 1.882-5 instead if that produces less U.S. taxable income in the taxpayer's particular circumstances

Paragraph 4

Paragraph 4 provides that profits shall be determined by the same method each year, unless there is good reason to change the method used. This rule assures consistent tax treatment over time for permanent establishments. It limits the ability of both the Contracting State and the enterprise to change accounting methods to be applied to the permanent establishment. It does not, however, restrict a Contracting State from imposing additional requirements, such as the rules under Code section 481, to prevent amounts from being duplicated or omitted following a change in accounting method.

Paragraph 5

Paragraph 5 states that the United States generally will not impose the excise tax on insurance policies issued by foreign insurers if the premiums on such policies are derived by a U.K. enterprise, whether or not the U.K. enterprise carries on business through a U.S. permanent establishment. The rule merely confirms the result that obtains under a combination of U.S. law and other provisions of the Convention. Because the excise tax is a covered tax under Article 2 (Taxes Covered), the United States may not, pursuant to paragraph 1 of Article 7, impose the tax on the income of any U.K. enterprise that is not attributable to a permanent establishment in the United States. Under Code section 4373, the tax also may not be imposed on any amount that is effectively connected with the conduct of a trade or business in the United States. Any amount attributable, under the Convention, to a permanent establishment in the United States also will be effectively connected with a U.S. trade or business. Therefore, the tax may not be imposed on any income of a U.K. enterprise that is attributable to a permanent establishment in the United States.

This relief from the excise tax, however, does not apply if the policies in question are entered into as part of a conduit arrangement, as defined in subparagraph (n) of paragraph 1 of Article 3 (General Definitions). Under current U.S. law, the anti-conduit regulations of section 1.881-3 do not apply with respect to the excise tax. Nevertheless, paragraph 5 of Article 7 of the Convention permits the United States to apply rules analogous to those of section 1.881-3 to transactions entered into as part of a conduit arrangement to avoid the imposition of the excise tax. If the transactions are entered into as part of a conduit arrangement to avoid the imposition of the excise tax, the excise tax may be applied unless the premiums are attributable to a permanent establishment maintained by a U.K. enterprise in the United States.

This anti-conduit rule is intended to apply to cases where a resident of a Contracting State receives an insurance premium, and then pays substantially all of that premium to a resident of a third state who would not be entitled to equivalent benefits if it received the insurance premium directly. Even if a transaction meets the structural requirements of the definition included in Article 3, it will not constitute a conduit arrangement if obtaining the increased benefits described in the preceding paragraphs was not the main purpose, or one of the main purposes, of the transaction. The United Kingdom and the United States agree that the terms "main purpose", used by the United Kingdom, and "principal purpose", used by the United States in its domestic law, are synonymous. Therefore, the United States will interpret the "main purpose" requirement of this rule in a manner consistent with the anti-conduit rules of regulation section 1.881-3, as it may be amended from time to time, and other U.S. domestic anti-abuse rules that look to the purposes of a transaction.

Because of the requirement that the arrangement have as one of its main purposes the avoidance of tax, this rule is somewhat narrower than the exception in other U.S. tax treaties that cover the insurance excise tax. Such other treaties impose the excise tax whenever a risk is reinsured with a person who would not be entitled to equivalent benefits, even if the reinsurance occurs in the ordinary course of business.

These rules are illustrated by the following examples:

Example 1. USCo is an insurance company resident in United States that is owned by a United Kingdom parent company, UKCo. XCo, an insurance company organized in a third country whose tax treaty with the United States does not cover the insurance excise tax, wants to enter into a reinsurance contract with USCo reinsuring 25 percent of all U.S. risks insured by USCo. However, XCo would like to avoid the excise tax on reinsurance policies issued by foreign persons. Accordingly, it proposes to UKCo that UKCo enter into a reinsurance contract with USCo, after which XCo will reinsure the risk ceded by USCo to UKCo. These transactions are entered into as proposed. As a result of these agreements, all or substantially all of the premiums paid by USCo to UKCo will be paid to XCo, and XCo will avoid the excise tax to which it would have been subject had it received the premium payments directly. Since one of

XCo's principle purposes in structuring the transaction in this way was to avoid the insurance excise tax, the arrangement constitutes a conduit arrangement, and UKCo will be subject to the U.S. insurance excise tax.

Example 2. The facts are the same as in Example 1, except that UKCo has a permanent establishment in the United States through which the transaction takes place. Since the premiums received from USCo are attributable to a permanent establishment which UKCo maintains in the United States, the United States will not impose an excise tax with respect to the policy between USCo and UKCo.

Paragraph 6

Paragraph 6 coordinates the provisions of Article 7 and other provisions of the Convention. Under this paragraph, when business profits include items of income that are dealt with separately under other articles of the Convention, the provisions of those articles will, except when they specifically provide to the contrary, take precedence over the provisions of Article 7. For example, the taxation of dividends will be determined by the rules of Article 10 (Dividends), and not by Article 7, except where, as provided in paragraph 6 of Article 10, the dividend is attributable to a permanent establishment. In the latter case the provisions of Article 7 apply. Thus, an enterprise of one State deriving dividends from the other State may not rely on Article 7 to exempt those dividends from tax at source if they are not attributable to a permanent establishment of the enterprise in the other State. By the same token, if the dividends are attributable to a permanent establishment in the other State, the dividends may be taxed on a net income basis at the source State full corporate tax rate, rather than on a gross basis under Article 10 (Dividends).

As provided in Article 8 (Shipping and Air Transport), income derived from shipping and air transport activities in international traffic described in that Article is taxable only in the country of residence of the enterprise regardless of whether it is attributable to a permanent establishment situated in the source State.

Paragraph 7

Paragraph 7 incorporates into the Convention the rule of Code section 864(c)(6). Like the Code section on which it is based, paragraph 7 provides that any income or gain attributable to a permanent establishment during its existence is taxable in the Contracting State where the permanent establishment is situated, even if the payment of that income or gain is deferred until after the permanent establishment ceases to exist. This rule applies with respect to Article 7 (Business Profits), paragraph 5 of Article 10 (Dividends), paragraph 3 of Article 11 (Interest), paragraph 3 of Article 12 (Royalties) and paragraph 2 of Article 22 (Other Income). A similar rule is incorporated into paragraph 3 of Article 13 (Gains).

The effect of this rule can be illustrated by the following example. Assume a company that is a resident of the United Kingdom and that maintains a permanent establishment in the United States winds up the permanent establishment's business and sells the permanent establishment's inventory and assets to a U.S. buyer at the end of year 1 in exchange for an interest-bearing installment obligation payable in full at the end of year 3. Despite the fact that Article 13's threshold requirement for U.S. taxation is not met in year 3 because the company has no permanent establishment in the United States, the United States may tax the deferred income payment recognized by the company in year 3.

Relation to Other Articles

This Article is subject to the saving clause of paragraph 4 of Article 1 (General Scope) of the Convention. Thus, if a citizen of the United States who is a resident of the United Kingdom under the treaty derives business profits from the United States that are not attributable to a permanent establishment in the United States, the United States may, subject to the special foreign tax credit rules of paragraph 6 of Article 24 (Relief from Double Taxation), tax those profits as part of the worldwide income of the citizen, notwithstanding the provision of paragraph 1 of this Article which would exempt the income from U.S. tax.

The benefits of this Article are also subject to Article 23 (Limitation on Benefits). Thus, an enterprise of the United Kingdom that derives income effectively connected with a U.S. trade or business may not claim the benefits of Article 7 unless the resident carrying on the enterprise qualifies for such benefits under Article 23.

Article 8 (Shipping and Air Transport)

This Article governs the taxation of profits from the operation of ships and aircraft in international traffic. The term "international traffic" is defined in subparagraph 1(d) of Article 3 (General Definitions). The taxation of gains from the alienation of ships, aircraft or containers is dealt with not in this Article but in paragraph 4 of Article 13 (Gains).

Paragraph 1

Paragraph 1 provides that profits derived by an enterprise of a Contracting State from the operation in international traffic of ships or aircraft are taxable only in that Contracting State. Because paragraph 6 of Article 7 (Business Profits) defers to Article 8 with respect to shipping income, such income derived by a resident of one of the Contracting States may not be taxed in the other State even if the enterprise has a permanent establishment in that other State. Thus, if a U.S. airline has a ticket office in the United Kingdom, the United Kingdom may not tax the airline's profits attributable to that office under Article 7. Since entities engaged in international transportation activities normally will have many permanent establishments in a number of countries, the rule avoids difficulties that would be encountered in attributing income to multiple permanent establishments if the income were covered by Article 7 (Business Profits).

Paragraph 2

The income from the operation of ships or aircraft in international traffic that is exempt from tax under paragraph 1 is defined in paragraph 2. In addition to income derived directly from the operation of ships and aircraft in international traffic, this definition also includes certain items of rental income that are closely related to those activities. First, income of an enterprise of a Contracting State from the rental of ships or aircraft on a full basis (*i.e.*, with crew) when such ships or aircraft are used in international traffic is income of the lessor from the operation of ships and aircraft in international traffic and, therefore, is exempt from tax in the other Contracting State under paragraph 1. Also, paragraph 2 encompasses income from the lease of ships or aircraft on a bareboat basis (*i.e.*, without crew) when the income is incidental to other income of the lessor from the operation of ships or aircraft in international traffic. Thus, the coverage of Article 8 of the Convention is generally consistent with Article 8 of the OECD Model although narrower than the U.S. Model, which also covers rentals from bareboat leasing that are not incidental to the operation of ships or aircraft by the lessee. The classes of income derived from the rental of ships and aircraft not included in this Article are included in Article 7.

Paragraph 2 also clarifies, consistent with the Commentary to Article 8 of the OECD Model, that income earned by an enterprise from the inland transport of property or passengers within either Contracting State falls within Article 8 if the transport is undertaken as part of the international transport of property or passengers by the enterprise. Thus, as confirmed by the notes, if a U.S. shipping company contracts to carry property from the United Kingdom to a U.S. city and, as part of that contract, it transports the property by truck from its point of origin to an airport in the United Kingdom (or it contracts with a trucking company to carry the property to the airport) the income earned by the U.S. shipping company from the overland leg of the journey would be taxable only in the United States. Similarly, Article 8 would apply to income from lighterage undertaken as part of the international transport of goods.

Finally, certain non-transport activities that are an integral part of the services performed by a transport company are understood to be covered in paragraph 1, though they are not specified in paragraph 2. These include, for example, the performance of some maintenance or catering services by one airline for another airline, if these services are incidental to the provision of those services by the airline for itself. Income earned by concessionaires, however, is not covered by Article 8. See paragraphs 7 through 10.1 of the Commentary to Article 8 of the OECD Model.

Paragraph 3

Under this paragraph, profits of an enterprise of a Contracting State from the use, maintenance or rental of containers (including equipment for their transport) that are used for the transport of goods in international traffic are exempt from tax in the other Contracting State. This result obtains under paragraph 3 regardless of whether the recipient of the income is engaged in the operation of ships or aircraft in international traffic, and regardless of whether the enterprise has a permanent establishment in the other Contracting State. By contrast, Article 8 of the OECD Model covers only income from the use, maintenance or rental of containers that is incidental to other income from international traffic.

Paragraph 4

This paragraph clarifies that the provisions of paragraphs 1 and 3 also apply to profits derived by an enterprise of a Contracting State from participation in a pool, joint business or international operating agency. This refers to various arrangements for international cooperation by carriers in shipping and air transport. For example, airlines from two countries may agree to share the transport of passengers between the two countries. They each will fly the same number of flights per week and share the revenues from that route equally, regardless of the number of passengers that each airline actually transports. Paragraph 4 makes clear that with respect to each carrier the Article excepts all the income earned by that carrier with respect to the pool, and not just the income derived directly by that carrier. This paragraph corresponds to paragraph 4 of Article 8 of the U.S. Model.

Relation to Other Articles

This Article is subject to the saving clause of paragraph 4 of Article 1 (General Scope) of the Convention. Thus, if a citizen of the United States who is a resident of the United Kingdom derives profits from the operation of ships or aircraft in international traffic, notwithstanding the exclusive residence country taxation in paragraph 1 of Article 8, the United States may, subject to the special foreign tax credit rules of paragraph 6 of Article 24 (Relief from Double Taxation), tax those profits as part of the worldwide income of the citizen. (This is an unlikely situation, however, because non-tax considerations (*e.g.*, insurance) generally result in shipping activities being carried on in corporate form.)

As with other benefits of the Convention, the benefit of exclusive residence country taxation under Article 8 is available to an enterprise only if it is entitled to benefits under Article 23 (Limitation on Benefits).

Article 9 (Associated Enterprises)

This Article incorporates in the Convention the arm's-length principle reflected in the U.S. domestic transfer pricing provisions, particularly Code section 482. It provides that when related enterprises engage in a transaction on terms that are not arm's-length, the Contracting States may make appropriate adjustments to the taxable income and tax liability of such related enterprises to reflect what the income and tax of these enterprises with respect to the transaction would have been had there been an arm's-length relationship between them.

Paragraph 1

This paragraph addresses the situation where an enterprise of a Contracting State is related to an enterprise of the other Contracting State, and there are arrangements or conditions imposed between the enterprises in their commercial or financial relations that are different from those that would have existed in the absence of the relationship. Under these circumstances, the Contracting States may adjust the income (or loss) of the enterprise to reflect what it would have been in the absence of such a relationship.

The paragraph identifies the relationships between enterprises that serve as a prerequisite to application of the Article. As the Commentary to Article 9 of the OECD Model makes clear, the necessary element in these relationships is effective control, which is also the standard for purposes of section 482. Thus, the Article applies if an enterprise of one State participates directly or indirectly in the management, control, or capital of the enterprise of the other State.

Also, the Article applies if any third person or persons participate directly or indirectly in the management, control, or capital of enterprises of different States. For this purpose, all types of control are included (*i.e.*, whether or not legally enforceable and however exercised or exercisable).

The fact that a transaction is entered into between such related enterprises does not, in and of itself, mean that a Contracting State may adjust the income (or loss) of one or both of the enterprises under the provisions of this Article. If the conditions of the transaction are consistent with those that would be made between independent persons, the income arising from that transaction should not be subject to adjustment under this Article.

Similarly, the fact that associated enterprises may have concluded arrangements, such as cost sharing arrangements or general services agreements, is not in itself an indication that the two enterprises have entered into a non-arm's-length transaction that should give rise to an adjustment under paragraph 1. Both related and unrelated parties enter into such arrangements (*e.g.*, joint venturers may share some development costs). As with any other kind of transaction, when related parties enter into an arrangement, the specific arrangement must be examined to see whether or not it meets the arm's-length standard. In the event that it does not, an appropriate adjustment may be made, which may include modifying the terms of the agreement or recharacterizing the transaction to reflect its substance.

It is understood that the "commensurate with income" standard for determining appropriate transfer prices for intangibles, added to Code section 482 by the Tax Reform Act of 1986, was designed to operate consistently with the arm's-length standard. The implementation of this standard in the section 482 regulations is in accordance with the general principles of paragraph 1 of Article 9 of the Convention, as interpreted by the OECD Transfer Pricing Guidelines.

It also is understood that the Contracting States preserve their rights to apply internal law provisions relating to adjustments between related parties. They also reserve the right to make adjustments in cases involving tax evasion or fraud. Such adjustments -- the distribution, apportionment, or allocation of income, deductions, credits or allowances -- are permitted even if they are different from, or go beyond, those authorized by paragraph 1 of the Article, as long as they accord with the general principles of paragraph 1 (*i.e.*, that the adjustment reflects what would have transpired had the related parties been acting at arm's length). For example, while paragraph 1 explicitly allows adjustments of deductions in computing taxable income, it does not deal with adjustments to tax credits. It does not, however, preclude such adjustments if they can be made under internal law. The OECD Model reaches the same result. See paragraph 4 of the Commentary to Article 9.

This Article also permits tax authorities to deal with thin capitalization issues. They may, in the context of Article 9, scrutinize more than the rate of interest charged on a loan between related persons. They also may examine the capital structure of an enterprise, whether a payment in respect of that loan should be treated as interest, and, if it is treated as interest, under what circumstances interest deductions should be allowed to the payer. Paragraph 2 of the Commentary to Article 9 of the OECD Model, together with the U.S. observation set forth in paragraph 15 thereof, sets forth a similar understanding of the scope of Article 9 in the context of thin capitalization.

Paragraph 2

When a Contracting State has made an adjustment that is consistent with the provisions of paragraph 1, and the other Contracting State agrees that the adjustment was appropriate to reflect arm's-length conditions, that other Contracting State is obligated to make a correlative adjustment (sometimes referred to as a "corresponding adjustment") to the tax liability of the related person in that other Contracting State. Although the OECD Model does not specify that the other Contracting State must agree with the initial adjustment before it is obligated to make the correlative adjustment, the Commentary makes clear that the paragraph is to be read that way.

As explained in the Commentary to Article 9 of the OECD Model, Article 9 leaves the treatment of "secondary adjustments" to the laws of the Contracting States. When an adjustment under Article 9 has been made, one of the parties will have in its possession funds that it would not have had at arm's length. The question arises as to how to treat these funds. In the United States the general practice is to treat such funds as a dividend or contribution to capital, depending on the relationship between the parties. Under certain circumstances, the parties may be permitted to restore the funds to the party that would have the funds at arm's length, and to establish an account payable pending restoration of the funds. See Rev. Proc. 99-32, 1999-2 C.B. 296.

The Contracting State making a secondary adjustment will take the other provisions of the Convention, where relevant, into account. For example, if the effect of a secondary adjustment is to treat a U.S. corporation as having made a distribution of profits to its parent corporation in the United Kingdom, the provisions of Article 10 (Dividends) will apply, and the United States may impose, where appropriate, a withholding tax on the dividend. Also, if under Article 24 (Relief from Double Taxation), the United Kingdom generally gives a credit for taxes paid with respect to such dividends, it would also be required to do so in this case.

As stated in the notes, it is understood that, if the amount of interest or royalties paid exceeds the amount that would have been paid in the absence of a relationship described in paragraph 4 of Article 11 or paragraph 4 of Article 12, a Contracting State generally will adjust the amount of deductible interest or royalties paid under the authority of Article 9 and make such other adjustments as are appropriate. If such an adjustment is made, however, then the Contracting State making such adjustment will not also impose its domestic rate of withholding tax with respect to such excess amount. Accordingly, if a U.K. company makes a royalty payment to its U.S. parent company, and the United Kingdom determines that the amount of the royalty exceeded an arm's-length amount, the United Kingdom will deny a deduction for the excess amount. It will not, however, treat the excess amount as a royalty subject to the 20 percent withholding rate applicable to royalties paid by U.K. companies.

The competent authorities are authorized by paragraph 3 of Article 26 (Mutual Agreement Procedure) to consult, if necessary, to resolve any differences in the application of these provisions. For example, there may be a disagreement over whether an adjustment made by a Contracting State under paragraph 1 was appropriate.

If a correlative adjustment is made under paragraph 2, it is to be implemented, pursuant to paragraph 2 of Article 26 (Mutual Agreement Procedure), notwithstanding any time limits or other procedural limitations in the law of the Contracting State making the adjustment. If a taxpayer has entered a closing agreement (or other written settlement) with the United States prior to bringing a case to the competent authorities, the U.S. competent authority will endeavor only to obtain a correlative adjustment from the United Kingdom. See, Rev. Proc. 2002-52, 2002-31 I.R.B. 242, Section 7.04.

Relationship to Other Articles

The saving clause of paragraph 4 of Article 1 (General Scope) does not apply to paragraph 2 of Article 9 by virtue of the exceptions to the saving clause in paragraph 5(a) of Article 1. Thus, even if the statute of limitations has run, a refund of tax can be made in order to implement a correlative adjustment. Statutory or procedural limitations, however, cannot be overridden to impose additional tax, because paragraph 2 of Article 1 provides that the Convention cannot restrict any statutory benefit.

Article 10 (Dividends)

Article 10 provides rules for the taxation of dividends paid by a company that is a resident of one Contracting State to a beneficial owner that is a resident of the other Contracting State. The article provides for full residence country taxation of such dividends and a limited source-State right to tax. Article 10 also provides rules for the imposition of a tax on branch profits by the State of source. Finally, the article prohibits a State from imposing taxes on a company resident in the other Contracting State, other than a branch profits tax, on undistributed earnings.

Paragraph 1

The right of a shareholder's country of residence to tax dividends arising in the source country is preserved by paragraph 1, which permits a Contracting State to tax its residents on dividends paid to them by a company that is a resident of the other Contracting State. For dividends from any other source paid to a resident, Article 22 (Other Income) grants the residence country exclusive taxing jurisdiction (other than for dividends attributable to a permanent establishment in the other State).

Paragraph 2

The State of source also may tax dividends beneficially owned by a resident of the other State, subject to the limitations of paragraphs 2 and 3. Paragraph 2 generally limits the rate of withholding tax in the State of source on dividends paid by a company resident in that State to 15 percent of the gross amount of the dividend. If, however, the beneficial owner of the dividend is a company resident in the other State and owns shares representing at least 10 percent of the voting power of the company paying the dividend, then the rate of withholding tax in the State of source is limited to 5 percent of the gross amount of the dividend. Indirect ownership of voting shares (through tiers of corporations) is taken into account for the purpose of determining eligibility for the 5 percent direct dividend rate of withholding tax. Shares are considered voting shares if they provide the power to elect, appoint or replace any person vested with the powers ordinarily exercised by the board of directors of a U.S. corporation.

The benefits of paragraph 2 may be granted at the time of payment by means of reduced rate of withholding tax at source. It also is consistent with the paragraph for tax to be withheld at the time of payment at full statutory rates, and the treaty benefit to be granted by means of a subsequent refund so long as such procedures are applied in a reasonable manner.

Paragraphs 2 and 3 do not affect the taxation of the profits out of which the dividends are paid. The taxation by a Contracting State of the income of its resident companies is governed by the internal law of the Contracting State, subject to the provisions of paragraph 4 of Article 25 (Non- Discrimination).

The term "beneficial owner" is not defined in the Convention, and is, therefore, defined as under the internal law of the country imposing tax (*i.e.*, the source country). The beneficial owner of the dividend for purposes of Article 10 is the person to which the dividend income is attributable for tax purposes under the laws of the source State. Thus, if a dividend paid by a corporation that is a resident of one of the States (as determined under Article 4 (Residence)) is received by a nominee or agent that is a resident of the other State on behalf of a person that is not a resident of that other State, the dividend is not entitled to the benefits of this Article. However, a dividend received by a nominee on behalf of a resident of that other State would be entitled to benefits. These limitations are confirmed by paragraph 12 of the OECD Commentary to Article 10. See also paragraph 24 of the Commentary to Article 1 of the OECD Model.

Companies holding shares through fiscally transparent entities such as partnerships are considered for purposes of this paragraph to hold their proportionate interest in the shares held by the intermediate entity. As a result, companies holding shares through such entities may be able to claim the benefits of subparagraph (a) under certain circumstances. The lower rate of withholding tax applies when the company's proportionate share of the shares held by the intermediate entity meets the 10 percent threshold. Whether this ownership threshold is satisfied may be difficult to determine and often will require an analysis of the partnership or trust agreement.

Paragraph 3

Paragraph 3 provides for exclusive residence country taxation (*i.e.,* a zero rate of withholding tax) with respect to certain dividends distributed by a company resident in one Contracting State to a resident in the other Contracting State. As described further below, the exemption is available with respect to certain intercompany dividends and with respect to dividends received by tax-exempt pension funds.

Subparagraph (a) of paragraph 3 reduces the rate of withholding tax to zero on dividends beneficially owned by a company that has owned directly at least 80 percent of the voting power of the company paying the dividend for the 12-month period ending on the date the dividend is declared.

Eligibility for the zero rate of withholding tax provided by subparagraph (a) is subject to an additional restriction which states that companies qualifying for treaty benefits by virtue of the active trade or business or ownership-base erosion test must have acquired shares representing 80 percent or more of the voting stock of the company paying the dividends prior to October 1, 1998. This restriction supplements those imposed under Article 23 (Limitation on Benefits), and is necessary because of the increased pressure on the Limitation on Benefits tests resulting from the fact that the Convention is one of the first U.S. tax treaties to provide for a zero rate of withholding on inter-company dividends. The test is intended to prevent companies from re-organizing in order to become eligible for the zero rate of withholding tax in circumstances where the Limitation on Benefits provision does not provide sufficient protection against treaty-shopping.

For example, assume that ThirdCo is a company resident in a third country, a member of the European Union other than the United Kingdom. ThirdCo owns directly 100 percent of the issued and outstanding voting stock of USCo, a U.S. company, and of UKCo, a U.K. company. UKCo is a substantial company that manufactures widgets; USCo distributes those widgets in the United States. If ThirdCo contributes to UKCo all the stock of USCo, dividends paid by USCo to UKCo would qualify for treaty benefits under the active trade or business test of Paragraph 4 of Article 23. However, allowing ThirdCo to qualify for the zero rate of withholding tax, which is not available to it under the third state's treaty with the United States (if any), would encourage treaty-shopping.

In order to prevent this type of treaty-shopping, the Convention imposes an additional holding requirement on companies that qualify for benefits only under the "active conduct of a trade or business" test (paragraph 4 of Article 23) or under the "ownership-base erosion" test (paragraph 2(f) of Article 23). For those companies, the zero rate of withholding tax is available only with respect to dividends received from companies that the recipient company owned, directly or indirectly, prior to October 1, 1998.

Accordingly, in the example above, UKCo will not qualify for the zero rate of withholding tax on dividends unless it owned USCo before October 1, 1998. If it did own USCo before October 1, 1998, then it will continue to qualify for the zero rate of withholding tax on dividends so long as it qualifies for benefits under at least one of the tests of Article 23. So, for example, if ThirdCo decided to get out of the widget business and sold its stock in UKCo to FWCo, a company that is resident in a country with which the United States does not have a tax treaty, UKCo would continue to qualify for the zero rate of withholding tax on dividends so long as it continued to meet the requirements of the active trade or business test of Article 23(4) or, possibly, the competent authority discretionary test of Article 23(6).

The result would be different under the "ownership-base erosion" test of Article 23(2)(f). For example, assume UKCo is a passive holding company owned by UK individuals, which was established in 1996 to hold the shares of USCo. UKCo qualifies for benefits only under the ownership-base erosion test of Article 23(2)(f). If the UK individuals sold their stock in UKCo to FWCo, UKCo would lose all the benefits accorded to residents of the UK under the Convention (including the zero withholding rate on dividends) because the company would no longer qualify for benefits under Article 23 (unless, of course, the U.S. competent authority were to grant benefits under Article 23(6)).

Other methods of qualifying under Limitation on Benefits do not raise the same concerns. Accordingly, a resident of a Contracting State that satisfies Limitation on Benefits by virtue of being a publicly-traded company or a subsidiary of a publicly-traded company does not have to meet the October 1, 1998 holding requirement. Thus, a U.K. resident company that meets the listing and trading requirements of Article 23(2)(c) will be entitled to the zero withholding rate on dividends no matter when it acquired the shares of the U.S. company (subject to the 12-month holding period requirement of Article 10(3)(a)).

Under Article 10(3)(a)(iii), a company that is a resident of a Contracting State may also qualify for the zero rate of withholding tax on dividends if it satisfies the derivative benefits test of paragraph 3 of Article 23, even if it acquired the U.S. company after September 30, 1998 (subject to the 12-month holding period requirement). Qualification for the zero rate of withholding tax through the application of the derivative benefits test currently is quite limited because of the definition of "equivalent beneficiary." Under that definition, as of the date of the signing of the Convention no U.K. subsidiary of a third-country company would qualify under the derivative benefits test of paragraph 3 of Article 23 because the United States had no other treaties with EU, EEA or NAFTA countries that reduce the rate of withholding tax on dividends to zero. Accordingly, a company could qualify for the zero rate of withholding tax pursuant to Article 10(3)(a)(iii) only if it is owned by seven or fewer U.S. or U.K. residents who fall within a limited category of "qualified persons." For example, it would apply to certain U.K. corporations that are closely-held by a few U.K. resident individuals or charities.

The provision would become more relevant if the United States were to enter into other treaties that reduce the rate of withholding tax on intercompany dividends to zero. For example, if the United States entered into a treaty with Country X, a member of the European Union, which eliminated the rate of withholding tax on intercompany dividends, then it would be possible for U.K. companies owned by companies resident in Country X to qualify for the benefits provided by subparagraph 3(a) of this Article by satisfying the requirements of the derivative benefits test of paragraph 3 of Article 23. The derivative benefits provision would also be relevant if the United Kingdom were to enact a positive rate of withholding tax on dividends.

The definition of "equivalent beneficiary" is also intended to ensure that certain joint ventures, not just wholly-owned subsidiaries, can qualify for benefits. For example, assume that the United States has entered into a treaty with Country X, a member of the European Union, that includes a provision identical to Article 10(3)(a). USCo is 100 percent owned by UKCo, which in turn is owned 49 percent by a U.K. publicly-traded company and 51 percent by XCo a publicly-traded company that is resident in Country X. The definition of "equivalent beneficiary" includes a rule of application that is intended to ensure that such joint ventures qualify for benefits. Under that rule, each of the shareholders is treated as owning the shares held by UKCo for purposes of determining whether it would be entitled to an equivalent rate of withholding tax. This rule is necessary because of the high ownership threshold for qualification for the zero rate of withholding tax. The standard rule is that the shareholders would be treated as owning only their proportionate share of the shares held by UKCo. If that rule were applied here, neither shareholder would be an equivalent beneficiary, since neither would meet the 80 percent ownership test with respect to USCo.

If a company does not qualify for the zero rate of withholding tax under any of the foregoing tests, it may request a determination from the relevant competent authority pursuant to paragraph 6 of Article 23. Benefits will be granted with respect to an item of income if the competent authority of the Contracting State in which the income arises determines that the establishment, acquisition or maintenance of such resident and the conduct of its operations did not have as one of its principal purposes the obtaining of benefits under the Convention.

In making its determination under Article 23(6) with respect to income arising in the United States, the U.S. competent authority will consider the obligations imposed upon the United Kingdom by its membership in the European Community. In particular, the United States will have regard to any legal requirements for the facilitation of the free movement of capital among Member States of the European Community. The competent authority will also consider the differing internal tax systems, tax incentive regimes and tax treaty policies of the relevant Member States.

For example, in the case above where UKCo was denied the zero rate of withholding tax because it was acquired by FWCo, the competent authority would consider whether FWCo were a resident of a Member State of the European Community or European Economic Area. If it were, that would be a factor in favor of a determination that UKCo is entitled to the benefits of the zero rate of withholding tax on dividends. This would be particularly true if the U.S. business was a relatively small portion of the business acquired. However, that positive factor could be outweighed by negative factors. One negative factor could be a determination by the U.S. competent authority that FWCo benefited from a tax incentive regime that eliminated any domestic taxation. The competent authority would also consider facts that might indicate that an acquisition was not undertaken "under ordinary business conditions" but instead was undertaken to acquire the U.K.-U.S. "bridge." These might include the fact that the U.K. company was acquired even though all or substantially all of the business activities acquired consisted of the U.S. business; the fact that existing U.S. operations were restructured in an attempt to benefit from the zero withholding rate; or the fact that FWCo was owned by residents of a country that is not a Member State of the European Union. Finally, another significant negative factor would be if the U.S. competent authority faced difficulties in learning the identity of FWCo's owners, such as an uncooperative taxpayer or legal barriers such as "economic espionage" or other limitations on the effective exchange of information in the country of which FWCo is a resident.

Subparagraph (b) of paragraph 3 provides for exclusive residence-State taxation (*i.e.*, a zero rate of withholding tax) for dividends beneficially owned by a pension scheme, as defined in Article 3(1)(o), provided that such dividends are not derived from the carrying on of a business, directly or indirectly, by the pension scheme.

Paragraph 4

Paragraph 4 modifies in particular cases the maximum rates of withholding tax at source provided in paragraphs 2 and 3. The first sentence of paragraph 4 provides that dividends paid by a pooled investment vehicle are not eligible for the 5 percent maximum rate of withholding tax in subparagraph (a) of paragraph 2, or the zero rate of withholding tax in subparagraph (a) of paragraph 3. As described below, the zero rate of withholding tax provided by subparagraph (b) of paragraph 3 (with respect to dividends paid to a pension plan) will be available with respect to dividends paid by a pooled investment vehicle in certain circumstances.

The term "pooled investment vehicle" is defined in subparagraph (b) of paragraph 10 of this Article. According to this definition, a pooled investment vehicle is a person with three attributes. First, its assets must consist wholly or mainly of real property, or of shares, securities or currencies, or of derivative contracts relating to shares, securities or currencies or real property. Second, its gross income must consist wholly or mainly of dividends, interest, gains from the alienation of assets and rents and other income and gains from the holding and alienation of real property. Third, it must be exempt from tax in respect of its income, profits or gains in the State of which it is a resident; or subject to tax at a special rate in that State; or entitled to a deduction for dividends paid to its shareholders in computing the amount of its income, profits or gains. This definition encompasses a U.S. regulated investment company ("RIC") or a U.S. real estate investment trust ("REIT").

The second sentence of paragraph 4 provides that the 15 percent maximum rate of withholding tax in subparagraph (b) of paragraph 2, and the zero rate of withholding tax of subparagraph (b) of paragraph 3 (with respect to dividends paid to pensions) are applicable to dividends paid by certain types of pooled investment vehicles. The pooled investment vehicles that qualify for reduced rates under this sentence include those with assets consisting wholly or mainly of shares, securities or currencies, or derivative contracts relating to shares, securities or currencies. Thus, dividends paid by REITs do not qualify under this sentence, but dividends paid by RICs qualify for the 15 percent maximum rate of withholding tax under the second sentence of paragraph 4 and the zero rate of withholding tax applicable to dividends paid to pension schemes.

The third sentence of paragraph 4 applies to pooled investment vehicle not covered by the second sentence of paragraph 4 (*e.g.*, REITs). Under this sentence, pension schemes will qualify for the zero rate of withholding tax with respect to dividends paid by such pooled investment schemes, provided that the pension scheme holds an interest of not more than 10 percent in the pooled investment vehicle. Other investors will qualify for the 15 percent maximum rate of withholding tax if one of three conditions is met. First, the dividend may qualify for the 15 percent rate of withholding tax if the beneficial owner is an individual holding an interest in the pooled investment vehicle of not more than 10 percent. Second, the dividend may qualify for the 15 percent rate of withholding tax if it is paid with respect to a class of stock that is publicly traded and the beneficial owner of the dividends is a person holding an interest of not more than 5 percent of any class of stock of the pooled investment vehicle. Third, the dividend may qualify for the 15 percent rate of withholding tax if the beneficial owner of the dividend is a person holding an interest in the pooled investment vehicle of not more than 10 percent and the vehicle is "diversified." The term "diversified" is defined in subparagraph (c) of paragraph 10.

Under this definition, a pooled investment vehicle such as a REIT will be considered diversified if the value of no single interest in real property exceeds 10 percent of the vehicle's total interests in real property. For purposes of this rule, foreclosure property is not considered an interest in real property. With respect to partnership interests held by a pooled investment vehicle, the vehicle will be treated as owning directly a proportionate share of the interests in real property held by the partnership.

The restrictions set out above are intended to prevent the use of these entities to gain inappropriate source-country tax benefits for certain shareholders resident in the other Contracting State. For example, a company resident in the United Kingdom that wishes to hold a diversified portfolio of U.S. corporate shares could hold the portfolio directly and pay a U.S. withholding tax at a rate of 15 percent on all of the dividends that it receives. Alternatively, it could hold the same diversified portfolio by purchasing 10 percent or more of the interests in a RIC. If the RIC is a pure conduit, there may be no U.S. tax cost to interposing the RIC in the chain of ownership. Absent the special rule in paragraph 4, such use of the RIC could transform portfolio dividends, taxable in the United States under the Convention at a 15 percent rate of withholding tax, into direct investment dividends taxable at a zero or 5 percent rate of withholding tax.

Similarly, a resident of the United Kingdom directly holding U.S. real property would pay U.S. tax either at a 30 percent rate of withholding tax on the gross income or at graduated rates on the net income. As in the preceding example, by placing the real property in a REIT, the investor could transform real estate income into dividend income, taxable at the rates provided in Article 10, significantly reducing the U.S. tax that otherwise would be imposed. Paragraph 4 prevents this result and thereby avoids a disparity between the taxation of direct real estate investments and real estate investments made through REIT conduits. In the cases covered by the exceptions, the holding in the REIT is not considered the equivalent of a direct holding in the underlying real property.

Paragraph 5

Paragraph 5 excludes from the general source country limitations under paragraph 2 and 3 dividends paid with respect to holdings that form part of the business property of a permanent establishment situated in the source country. Such dividends will be taxed on a net basis using the rates and rules of taxation generally applicable to residents of the State in which the permanent establishment is located, as modified by the Convention. An example of dividends paid with respect to the business property of a permanent establishment would be dividends derived by a dealer in stock or securities from stock or securities that the dealer held for sale to customers.

In the case of a permanent establishment that once existed in the State but that no longer exists, the provisions of paragraph 5 also apply, by virtue of paragraph 7 of Article 7 (Business

Profits), to dividends that would be attributable to such a permanent establishment if it did exist in the year of payment or accrual. See the Technical Explanation of paragraph 7 of Article 7.

Paragraph 6

A State's right to tax dividends paid by a company that is a resident of the other State is restricted by paragraph 6 to cases in which the dividends are paid to a resident of that State or are attributable to a permanent establishment in that State. Thus, a State may not impose a "secondary" withholding tax on dividends paid by a nonresident company out of earnings and profits from that State. In the case of the United States, paragraph 6, therefore, overrides the ability to impose taxes under sections 871 and 882(a) on dividends paid by foreign corporations that have a U.S. source under section 861(a)(2)(B).

The paragraph also restricts a State's right to impose corporate level taxes on undistributed profits, other than a branch profits tax. The accumulated earnings tax and the personal holding company taxes are taxes covered in Article 2 (Taxes Covered). Accordingly, under the provisions of Article 7 (Business Profits), the United States may not impose those taxes on the income of a resident of the other State except to the extent that income is attributable to a permanent establishment in the United States. Paragraph 6 further confirms the restriction on the U.S. authority to impose those taxes. The paragraph does not restrict a State's right to tax its resident shareholders on undistributed earnings of a corporation resident in the other State. Thus, the U.S. authority to impose the foreign personal holding company tax, its taxes on subpart F income and on an increase in earnings invested in U.S. property, and its tax on income of a passive foreign investment company that is a qualified electing fund is in no way restricted by this provision.

Paragraph 7

Paragraph 7 permits a State to impose a branch profits tax on a company resident in the other State. The tax is in addition to other taxes permitted by the Convention. The term "company" is defined in Article 3.

A State may impose a branch profits tax on a corporation if the corporation has income attributable to a permanent establishment in that State, derives income from real property in that State that is taxed on a net basis under Article 6 (Income from Real Property), or realizes gains taxable in that State under paragraph 1 of Article 13 (Gains). The tax is limited, however, to the aforementioned items of income that are included in the "dividend equivalent amount."

As stated in the notes, the term "dividend equivalent amount" for any year approximates the dividend that a U.S. branch office would have paid during the year if the branch had been operated as a separate U.S. subsidiary company. Generally, the dividend equivalent amount for a particular year is the income described above that is included in the corporation's effectively connected earnings and profits for that year, after payment of the corporate tax under Articles 6 (Income from Real Property), 7 (Business Profits) or 13 (Gains), reduced for any increase in the branch's U.S. net equity during the year or increased for any reduction in its U.S. net equity during the year. U.S. net equity is U.S. assets less U.S. liabilities. See Treas. Reg. section 1.884-

1. The United States may not impose its branch profits tax on the business profits of a corporation resident in the United Kingdom that are effectively connected with a U.S. trade or business but that are not attributable to a permanent establishment and are not otherwise subject to U.S. taxation under Article 6 (Income from Real Property) or paragraph 1 of Article 13 (Gains).

The United Kingdom currently does not impose a branch profits tax. If the United Kingdom were to impose such a tax, the base of such a tax would be limited to an amount analogous to the U.S. dividend equivalent.

The branch profits tax will not be imposed, however, if certain requirements are met. In general, these requirements provide rules for a branch that parallel the rules for when a dividend paid by a subsidiary will be subject to exclusive residence-country taxation (i.e., a zero rate of withholding tax). Accordingly, the branch profits tax may not be imposed in the case of a company which, before October 1, 1998, was engaged in activities constituting a permanent establishment (whether or not the permanent establishment was actually profitable during that period) or to income or gains that are of a type that would be subject to the provisions of Article 6 or paragraph 1 of Article 13. In addition, paragraph 7 does not apply to a company which is a qualified person by reason of subparagraph (c) of paragraph 2 of Article 23 (Limitation on Benefits) (*i.e.*, a publicly-traded company). Finally, paragraph 7 does not apply to a company entitled to benefits with respect to dividends under paragraph 3 (the derivative benefits test) or paragraph 6 (the competent authority discretionary test) of Article 23 with respect to the dividend equivalent amount.

Thus, for example, if a U.K. company would be subject to the branch profits tax with respect to profits attributable to a U.S. branch and not reinvested in that branch, paragraph 7 may apply to eliminate the branch profits tax if that branch was established in the United States before October 1, 1998 and the other requirements of the Convention (e.g., Limitation on Benefits) are met. If, by contrast, a U.K. company that did not have a branch in the United States before October 1, 1998, takes over after October 1, 1998, the activities of a branch belonging to a third party, then the branch profits tax would apply, unless the U.K. company is a qualified person under subparagraph (c) of paragraph 2 of Article 23 or entitled to benefits under paragraph 3 or paragraph 6 of that Article.

Moreover, the transfer of assets from a branch that meets the requirements for an exemption under paragraph 7 into a subsidiary that meets the requirements of paragraph 3 should not change this result. Accordingly, in that case, it is expected that the U.S. competent authority will exercise its discretion to treat the new parent-subsidiary group as qualified for the zero rate of withholding tax as well, so long as the U.K. parent meets the 80-percent ownership requirement of paragraph 3(a) of Article 10 with respect to the subsidiary.

Paragraph 8

Paragraph 8 provides that the branch profits tax permitted by paragraph 7 shall not be imposed at a rate of withholding tax exceeding the maximum direct investment dividend rate of withholding tax of five percent. This rule will apply only if the conditions described above in relation to paragraph 7 are not met.

Paragraph 9

Paragraph 9 provides that Article 10 will not apply to any dividend paid under, or as part of, a conduit arrangement. The term "conduit arrangement" is defined in subparagraph (n) of paragraph 1 of Article 3 (General Definitions). As discussed in the Technical Explanation to that provision, the United States will interpret this rule co-extensively and consistently with U.S. domestic law, including in particular the rules of regulation section 1.881-3 and other regulations adopted under the authority of section 7701(l) of the Code.

Paragraph 10

Paragraph 10 provides definitions of certain terms used in Article 10. Subparagraph (a) defines the term "dividends" broadly and flexibly. The definition is intended to cover all arrangements that yield a return on an equity investment in a corporation as determined under the tax law of the State of source, as well as arrangements that might be developed in the future.

The term "dividends" includes income from shares, or other corporate rights that are not treated as debt under the law of the source State, that participate in the profits of the company. The term also includes income that is subjected to the same tax treatment as income from shares by the law of the State of source. Thus, a constructive dividend that results from a non-arm's length transaction between a corporation and a related party is a dividend. Finally, a payment denominated as interest that is made by a thinly capitalized corporation may be treated as a dividend to the extent that the debt is recharacterized as equity under the laws of the source State.

In the case of the United States, the term dividend includes amounts treated as a dividend under U.S. law upon the sale or redemption of shares or upon a transfer of shares in a reorganization. See, *e.g.*, Rev. Rul. 92-85, 1992-2 C.B. 69 (sale of foreign subsidiary's stock to U.S. sister company is a deemed dividend to extent of subsidiary's and sister's earnings and profits). Further, a distribution from a U.S. publicly traded limited partnership, which is taxed as a corporation under U.S. law, is a dividend for purposes of Article 10. However, a distribution by a limited liability company is not characterized by the United States as a dividend and, therefore, is not a dividend for purposes of Article 10, provided the limited liability company is not characterized as an association taxable as a corporation under U.S. law.

Subparagraphs (b) and (c) define the terms "pooled investment vehicle" and "diversified," respectively. These terms are discussed above in connection with paragraph 4 of Article 10.

Relation to Other Articles

Notwithstanding the foregoing limitations on source country taxation of dividends, the saving clause of paragraph 4 of Article 1 (General Scope) permits the United States to tax dividends received by its residents and citizens, subject to the special foreign tax credit rules of paragraph 6 of Article 24 (Relief from Double Taxation), as if the Convention had not come into effect.

The benefits of this Article are also subject to the provisions of Article 23 (Limitation on Benefits). Thus, if a resident of the United Kingdom is the beneficial owner of dividends paid by a U.S. company, the shareholder must qualify for treaty benefits under at least one of the tests of Article 23 in order to receive the benefits of this Article.

Article 11 (Interest)

Article 11 provides rules for the taxation of interest arising in one Contracting State and paid to a beneficial owner that is a resident of the other Contracting State.

Paragraph 1

Paragraph 1 generally grants to the State of residence the exclusive right to tax interest beneficially owned by its residents and arising in the other Contracting State.

The term "beneficial owner" is not defined in the Convention, and is, therefore, defined under the internal law of the State of source. The beneficial owner of the interest for purposes of Article 11 is the person to which the interest income is attributable for tax purposes under the laws of the State of source. Thus, if interest arising in a Contracting State is received by a nominee or agent that is a resident of the other State on behalf of a person that is not a resident of that other State, the interest is not entitled to the benefits of Article 11. However, interest received by a nominee on behalf of a resident of that other State would be entitled to benefits. These limitations are confirmed by paragraph 8 of the OECD Commentary to Article 11. See also paragraph 24 of the OECD Commentary to Article 1.

Paragraph 2

The term "interest" as used in Article 11 is defined in paragraph 2 to include, *inter alia*, income from debt claims of every kind, whether or not secured by a mortgage. Penalty charges for late payment are excluded from the definition of interest. Interest that is paid or accrued subject to a contingency is within the ambit of Article 11. This includes income from a debt obligation carrying the right to participate in profits. The term does not, however, include amounts that are treated as dividends under Article 10 (Dividends).

The term interest also includes amounts subject to the same tax treatment as income from money lent under the law of the State in which the income arises. Thus, for purposes of the Convention, amounts that the United States will treat as interest include (i) the difference between the issue price and the stated redemption price at maturity of a debt instrument (*i.e.*, original issue discount ("OID")), which may be wholly or partially realized on the disposition of a debt instrument (section 1273), (ii) amounts that are imputed interest on a deferred sales contract (section 483), (iii) amounts treated as interest or OID under the stripped bond rules (section 1286), (iv) amounts treated as original issue discount under the below-market interest rate rules (section 7872), (v) a partner's distributive share of a partnership's interest income (section 702), (vi) the interest portion of periodic payments made under a "finance lease" or similar contractual arrangement that in substance is a borrowing by the nominal lessee to finance the acquisition of property, (vii) amounts included in the income of a holder of a residual interest in a REMIC (section 860E), because these amounts generally are subject to the same taxation treatment as interest under U.S. tax law, and (viii) interest with respect to notional principal contracts that are recharacterized as loans because of a "substantial non-periodic payment."

Paragraph 3

Paragraph 3 provides an exception to the exclusive residence taxation rule of paragraph 1 in cases where the beneficial owner of the interest carries on business through a permanent establishment in the State of source and the interest is attributable to that permanent establishment. In such cases the provisions of Article 7 (Business Profits) will apply and the State of source will retain the right to impose tax on such interest income.

In the case of a permanent establishment that once existed in the State but that no longer exists, the provisions of paragraph 3 also apply, by virtue of paragraph 7 of Article 7 (Business Profits), to interest that would be attributable to such a permanent establishment if it did exist in the year of payment or accrual. See the Technical Explanation of paragraph 7 of Article 7.

Paragraph 4

Paragraph 4 provides that, in cases involving special relationships between persons, Article 11 applies only to that portion of the total interest payments between those persons that would have been made absent such special relationships (*i.e.*, an arm's-length interest payment). Any excess amount of interest paid remains taxable according to the laws of the United States and the United Kingdom, respectively, with due regard to the other provisions of the Convention. Thus, if the excess amount would be treated under the source country's law as a distribution of profits by a corporation, such amount would be taxed as a dividend rather than as interest, but the tax would be subject, if appropriate, to the rate limitations of Article 10 (Dividends).

The notes further clarify the application of this paragraph. As stated there, if the amount of interest paid exceeds the amount that would have been paid in the absence of a relationship described in paragraph 4 of Article 11, a Contracting State generally will adjust the amount of deductible interest paid under the authority of Article 9 and make such other adjustments as are appropriate. If such an adjustment is made, however, then the Contracting State making such adjustment will not also impose its domestic rate of withholding tax with respect to such excess amount. Accordingly, if a U.K. company makes an interest payment to its U.S. parent company, and the United Kingdom determines that the amount of the interest exceeded an arm's-length amount, the United Kingdom will deny a deduction for the excess amount. It will not, however, treat the excess amount as interest subject to the 20 percent withholding rate applicable to interest paid by U.K. companies.

The term "special relationship" is not defined in the Convention. In applying this paragraph the United States considers the term to include the relationships described in Article 9

(Associated Enterprises), which in turn correspond to the definition of "control" for purposes of section 482 of the Code.

This paragraph does not address cases where, owing to a special relationship between the payer and the beneficial owner or between both of them and some other person, the amount of the interest is less than an arm's-length amount. In those cases a transaction may be characterized to reflect its substance and interest may be imputed consistent with the definition of interest in paragraph 2. Consistent with Article 9 (Associated Enterprises), the United States would apply section 482 or 7872 of the Code to determine the amount of imputed interest in those cases.

Paragraph 5

Paragraph 5 provides an anti-abuse exception to paragraph 1 for so-called "contingent interest." Under subparagraph (a) of paragraph 5, interest arising in one of the Contracting States that is determined by reference to the receipts, sales, income, profits or other cash flow of the debtor or a related person, to any change in the value of any property of the debtor or a related person or to any dividend, partnership distribution or similar payment made by the debtor to a related person, also may be taxed in the Contracting State in which it arises, and according to the laws of that State. If the beneficial owner is a resident of the other Contracting State, however, the gross amount of the interest may be taxed at a rate not exceeding 15 percent (the rate prescribed in subparagraph (b) of paragraph 2 of Article 10 (Dividends)).

Subparagraph (b) of paragraph 5 provides an exception to the anti-abuse rule stated in subparagraph (a). Under subparagraph (b), the anti-abuse rule will not apply to any interest solely because it is paid under an arrangement providing for a reduction or an increase in payment amount in the event of an improvement or deterioration, respectively, in the factors by reference to which the amount of interest payable is determined. Thus, for example, interest will not become contingent interest solely by virtue of a provision in the agreement that calls for an increase in the rate charged upon the deterioration of the credit position of the borrower.

Paragraph 6

Paragraph 6 provides an anti-abuse exception to paragraph 1 for excess inclusions from U.S. real estate mortgage investment conduits ("REMICs"). Paragraph 6 serves as a backstop to Code section 860G(b). That section generally requires that a foreign person holding a residual interest in a REMIC take into account for U.S. tax purposes "any excess inclusion" and "amounts includible . . . [under the REMIC provisions] when paid or distributed (or when the interest is disposed of) . . . ."

Without a full tax at source, non-U.S. transferees of residual interests would have a competitive advantage over U.S. transferees at the time these interests are initially offered. Absent this rule, the United States would suffer a revenue loss with respect to mortgages held in a REMIC because of opportunities for tax avoidance created by differences in the timing of taxable and economic income produced by such interests. In many cases, the transfer to the foreign person is simply disregarded under Reg. § 1.860G-3. Paragraph 6 also serves to indicate that excess inclusions from REMICs are not considered "other income" subject to Article 22 (Other Income) of the Convention.

Paragraph 6 is analogous to subparagraph (b) of paragraph 5 of the U.S. Model, except that in the Convention the provision is drafted to apply bilaterally. Thus, for example, paragraph 6 does not refer to the long-term Federal rate used to determine the amount of an excess inclusion, but rather to "the return on comparable debt instruments as specified by the domestic law of that State." Nevertheless, for U.S. tax purposes, the withholding tax imposed "to the extent that the amount of interest paid exceeds the return on comparable debt instruments as specified by the domestic law of that State" is the withholding tax that would be imposed upon an excess inclusion with respect to a residual interest in a REMIC under section 860G(b).

Paragraph 7

Paragraph 7 provides that Article 11 will not apply to any interest paid under, or as part of, a conduit arrangement. The term "conduit arrangement" is defined in subparagraph (n) of paragraph 1 of Article 3 (General Definitions). As discussed in the Technical Explanation to that provision, the United States will interpret this rule co-extensively and consistently with U.S. domestic law, including in particular the rules of regulation section 1.881-3 and other regulations adopted under the authority of section 7701(l) of the Code.

Relation to Other Articles

Notwithstanding the foregoing limitations on source country taxation of interest, the saving clause of paragraph 4 of Article 1 (General Scope) permits the United States to tax its residents and citizens, subject to the special foreign tax credit rules of paragraph 6 of Article 24 (Relief from Double Taxation), as if the Convention had not come into force.

The benefits of this Article are also subject to the provisions of Article 23 (Limitation on Benefits). Thus, if a resident of the United Kingdom is the beneficial owner of interest paid by a U.S. corporation, the shareholder must qualify for treaty benefits under at least one of the tests of Article 23 in order to receive the benefits of this Article.

Article 12 (Royalties)

Article 12 provides rules for the taxation of royalties arising in one Contracting State and paid to a beneficial owner that is a resident of the other Contracting State.

Paragraph 1

Paragraph 1 generally grants to the State of residence the exclusive right to tax royalties beneficially owned by its residents and arising in the other Contracting State.

The term "beneficial owner" is not defined in the Convention, and is, therefore, defined under the internal law of the State of source. The beneficial owner of the royalty for purposes of Article 12 is the person to which the royalty income is attributable for tax purposes under the laws of the State of source. Thus, if a royalty arising in a Contracting State is received by a nominee or agent that is a resident of the other State on behalf of a person that is not a resident of that other State, the royalty is not entitled to the benefits of Article 12. However, a royalty received by a nominee on behalf of a resident of that other State would be entitled to benefits. These limitations are confirmed by paragraph 4 of the OECD Commentary to Article 12. See also paragraph 24 of the OECD Commentary to Article 1.

Paragraph 2

Paragraph 2 defines the term "royalties," as used in Article 12, to include any consideration for the use of, or the right to use, any copyright of literary, artistic, scientific or other work (such as computer software and cinematographic films); for the use of, or the right to use, any patent, trademark, design or model, plan, secret formula or process, or other like right or property; or for information concerning industrial, commercial, or scientific experience. The term "royalties" also includes gain derived from the alienation of any right or property that would give rise to royalties, to the extent the gain is contingent on the productivity, use, or further alienation thereof. Gains that are not so contingent are dealt with under Article 13 (Gains). The term "royalties," however, does not include income from leasing personal property.

The term royalties is defined in the Convention and therefore is generally independent of domestic law. Certain terms used in the definition are not defined in the Convention, but these may be defined under domestic tax law. For example, the term "secret process or formulas" is found in the Code, and its meaning has been elaborated in the context of sections 351 and 367. See Rev. Rul. 55- 17, 1955-1 C.B. 388; Rev. Rul. 64-56, 1964-1 C.B. 133; Rev. Proc. 69- 19, 1969-2 C.B. 301.

Consideration for the use or right to use cinematographic films, or works on film, tape, or other means of reproduction in radio or television broadcasting is specifically included in the definition of royalties. It is intended that, with respect to any subsequent technological advances in the field of radio or television broadcasting, consideration received for the use of such technology will also be included in the definition of royalties.

If an artist who is resident in one Contracting State records a performance in the other Contracting State, retains a copyrighted interest in a recording, and receives payments for the right to use the recording based on the sale or public playing of the recording, then the right of such other Contracting State to tax those payments is governed by Article 12. See Boulez v. Commissioner, 83 T.C. 584 (1984), aff'd, 810 F.2d 209 (D.C. Cir. 1986). By contrast, if the artist earns in the other Contracting State income covered by Article 16 (Entertainers and Sportsmen), for example, endorsement income from the artist's attendance at a film screening, and if such income also is attributable to one of the rights described in Article 12 (*e.g.*, the use of the artist's photograph in promoting the screening), Article 16 and not Article 12 is applicable to such income.

Computer software generally is protected by copyright laws around the world. Under the Convention, consideration received for the use, or the right to use, computer software is treated either as royalties or as business profits, depending on the facts and circumstances of the transaction giving rise to the payment.

The primary factor in determining whether consideration received for the use, or the right to use, computer software is treated as royalties or as business profits is the nature of the rights transferred. See Treas. Reg. section 1.861-18. The fact that the transaction is characterized as a license for copyright law purposes is not dispositive. For example, a typical retail sale of "shrink wrap" software generally will not be considered to give rise to royalty income, even though for copyright law purposes it may be characterized as a license.

The means by which the computer software is transferred are not relevant for purposes of the analysis. Consequently, if software is electronically transferred but the rights obtained by the transferee are substantially equivalent to rights in a program copy, the payment will be considered business profits.

The term "industrial, commercial, or scientific experience" (sometimes referred to as "know-how") has the meaning ascribed to it in paragraph 11 of the Commentary to Article 12 of the OECD Model. Consistent with that meaning, the term may include information that is ancillary to a right otherwise giving rise to royalties, such as a patent or secret process.

Know-how also may include, in limited cases, technical information that is conveyed through technical or consultancy services. It does not include general educational training of the user's employees, nor does it include information developed especially for the user, such as a technical plan or design developed according to the user's specifications. Thus, as provided in paragraph 11 of the Commentary to Article 12 of the OECD Model, the term "royalties" does not include payments received as consideration for after-sales service, for services rendered by a seller to a purchaser under a guarantee, or for pure technical assistance.

The term "royalties" also does not include payments for professional services (such as architectural, engineering, legal, managerial, medical, software development services). For example, income from the design of a refinery by an engineer (even if the engineer employed know-how in the process of rendering the design) or the production of a legal brief by a lawyer is not income from the transfer of know-how taxable under Article 12, but is income from services taxable under either Article 7 (Business Profits) or Article 14 (Income from Employment). Professional services may be embodied in property that gives rise to royalties, however. Thus, if a professional contracts to develop patentable property and retains rights in the resulting property under the development contract, subsequent license payments made for those rights would be royalties.

Paragraph 3

Paragraph 3 provides an exception to the rules of paragraph 1 that limit the rate of source country taxation of royalties. This paragraph applies in cases where the beneficial owner of the royalties carries on business through a permanent establishment in the State of source and the royalties are attributable to that permanent establishment. In such cases the provisions of Article 7 (Business Profits) will apply.

The provisions of paragraph 7 of Article 7 (Business Profits) apply to this paragraph. For example, royalty income that is attributable to a permanent establishment and that accrues during the existence of the permanent establishment, but is received after the permanent establishment no longer exists, remains taxable under the provisions of Article 7 (Business Profits), and not under this Article.

Paragraph 4

Paragraph 4 provides that in cases involving special relationships between the payer and beneficial owner of royalties, Article 12 applies only to the extent the royalties would have been paid absent such special relationships (*i.e.*, an arm's-length royalty). Any excess amount of royalties paid remains taxable according to the laws of the two Contracting States with due regard to the other provisions of the Convention. If, for example, the excess amount is treated as a distribution of corporate profits under domestic law, such excess amount would be taxed as a dividend rather than as royalties, but the tax imposed on the dividend payment would be subject to the rate limitations of Article 10 (Dividends).

The notes further clarify the application of this paragraph. As stated there, if the amount of royalties paid exceeds the amount that would have been paid in the absence of a relationship described in paragraph 4 of Article 12, a Contracting State generally will adjust the amount of deductible royalties paid under the authority of Article 9 and make such other adjustments as are appropriate. If such an adjustment is made, however, then the Contracting State making such adjustment will not also impose its domestic rate of withholding tax with respect to such excess amount. Accordingly, if a U.K. company makes a royalty payment to its U.S. parent company, and the United Kingdom determines that the amount of the royalty exceeded an arm's-length amount, the United Kingdom will deny a deduction for the excess amount. It will not, however, treat the excess amount as a royalty subject to the 22 percent withholding rate applicable to royalties paid by U.K. companies.

Paragraph 5

Paragraph 5 provides that Article 12 will not apply to any royalty paid under, or as part of, a conduit arrangement. The term "conduit arrangement" is defined in subparagraph (n) of paragraph 1 of Article 3 (General Definitions). As discussed in the Technical Explanation to that provision, the United States will interpret this rule co-extensively and consistently with U.S. domestic law, including in particular the rules of regulation section 1.881-3 and other regulations adopted under the authority of section 7701(l) of the Code.

Relation to Other Articles

Notwithstanding the foregoing limitations on source country taxation of royalties, the saving clause of paragraph 4 of Article 1 (General Scope) permits the United States to tax its residents and citizens, subject to the special foreign tax credit rules of paragraph 6 of Article 24 (Relief from Double Taxation), as if the Convention had not come into force.

The benefits of this Article are also subject to the provisions of Article 23 (Limitation on Benefits). Thus, if a resident of the United Kingdom is the beneficial owner of royalties paid by a U.S. corporation, the shareholder must qualify for treaty benefits under at least one of the tests of Article 23 in order to receive the benefits of this Article.

Article 13 (Gains)

Article 13 assigns either primary or exclusive taxing jurisdiction over gains from the alienation of property to the State of residence or the State of source and defines the terms necessary to apply the Article.

Paragraph 1

Paragraph 1 of Article 13 preserves the non-exclusive right of the State of source to tax gains attributable to the alienation of real property situated in that State. The paragraph therefore permits the United States to apply section 897 of the Code to tax gains derived by a resident of the United Kingdom that are attributable to the alienation of real property situated in the United States (as defined in paragraph 2). Gains attributable to the alienation of real property include gains from any other property that is treated as a real property interest within the meaning of paragraph 2.

Paragraph 2

This paragraph defines the term "real property situated in the other Contracting State" to include assets that might not be considered real property under the definition of subparagraph 1(m) of Article 3 (Definitions), which is limited to interests in the real property itself. For example, under subparagraph (a), the term "real property situated in the other Contracting State" includes exploration and exploitation rights with respect to the sea bed and sub-soil of that other State and their natural resources, including rights to interests in or the benefit of such assets. In the case of the United States, such rights would be treated as real property pursuant to section 897 so the specific rule in Article 13 is not necessary. Such rights would not be treated as real property under U.K. domestic law, so the rule is necessary to provide consistent treatment.

Under subparagraph (b), the term "real property situated in the other Contracting State" includes a "United States real property interest," when the United States is the other Contracting State under paragraph 1. The term "United States real property interest" includes shares in a U.S. company that owns sufficient U.S. real property interests to satisfy an asset-ratio test on certain testing dates. *See* I.R.C. § 897(c). The term "United States real property interest" also encompasses an interest in a foreign company that has elected to be treated as a U.S. company for this purpose. *See* I.R.C. § 897(i). In applying paragraph 1 the United States will look through capital gain distributions made by a REIT. Accordingly, distributions made by a REIT are taxable under paragraph 1 of Article 13 (not under Article 10 (Dividends)) when they are attributable to gains derived from the alienation of real property.

Under subparagraph (c), the term "real property situated in the other Contracting State" includes, when the United Kingdom is the other Contracting State, shares, including rights to acquire shares, other than shares in which there is regular trading on a stock exchange, deriving their value or the greater part of their value directly or indirectly from real property situated in the United Kingdom. The term also includes an interest in a partnership or trust, to the extent the assets of the partnership or trust consist of real property situated in the United Kingdom, or of shares referred to in the preceding sentence.

Paragraph 3

Paragraph 3 of Article 13 deals with the taxation of certain gains from the alienation of property, other than real property, forming part of the business property of a permanent establishment that an enterprise of a Contracting State has in the other Contracting State. This also includes gains from the alienation of such a permanent establishment (alone or with the whole enterprise). Such gains may be taxed in the State in which the permanent establishment is located.

A resident of the United Kingdom that is a partner in a partnership doing business in the United States generally will have a permanent establishment in the United States as a result of the activities of the partnership, assuming that the activities of the partnership rise to the level of a permanent establishment. Rev. Rul. 91-32, 1991-1 C.B. 107. Further, under paragraph 3, the United States generally may tax a partner's distributive share of income realized by a partnership on the disposition of personal (movable) property forming part of the business property of the partnership in the United States.

The gains subject to paragraph 3 may be taxed in the State in which the permanent establishment is located, regardless of whether the permanent establishment exists at the time of the alienation. This rule incorporates the rule of section 864(c)(6) of the Code. Accordingly, income that is attributable to a permanent establishment, but that is deferred and received after the permanent establishment no longer exists, may nevertheless be taxed by the State in which the permanent establishment was located.

Paragraph 4

This paragraph limits the taxing jurisdiction of the State of source with respect to gains from the alienation of ships or aircraft operated in international traffic by the enterprise alienating the ship or aircraft, from containers used in international traffic, and from property (other than real property) pertaining to the operation or use of such ships, aircraft, or containers.

Under paragraph 4, such income is taxable only in the Contracting State in which the alienator is resident. Notwithstanding paragraph 3, the rules of this paragraph apply even if the income is attributable to a permanent establishment maintained by the enterprise in the other Contracting State. This result is consistent with the allocation of taxing rights under Article 8 (Shipping and Air Transport).

Paragraph 5

Paragraph 5 grants to the State of residence of the alienator the exclusive right to tax gains from the alienation of property other than property referred to in paragraphs 1 through 4. For example, gain derived from shares (other than shares described in paragraphs 2 or 3), debt instruments and various financial instruments, may be taxed only in the State of residence, to the extent such income is not otherwise characterized as income taxable under another article (*e.g.*, Article 10 (Dividends) or Article 11 (Interest)). Similarly, gain derived from the alienation of tangible personal property, other than tangible personal property described in paragraph 3, may be taxed only in the State of residence of the alienator. Gain derived from the alienation of any property, such as a patent or copyright, that produces income taxable under Article 12 (Royalties) is taxable under Article 12 and not under this article, provided that such gain is of the type described in subparagraph 3(b) of Article 12 (*i.e.*, it is contingent on the productivity, use, or disposition of the property). Sales by a resident of a Contracting State of real property located in a third state are not taxable in the other Contracting State, even if the sale is attributable to a permanent establishment located in the other Contracting State.

Paragraph 6

Paragraph 6 allows each Contracting State to tax gains derived by certain non-residents who used to be residents of that Contracting State. The rule is included in the Convention in order to allow the United Kingdom to apply its domestic law regarding such sales. Under U.K. law, a former resident who re-establishes residence in the United Kingdom within five years will remain subject to tax in the United Kingdom on any gains realized during the period of non-residence. The analogous U.S. rules of section 877 are preserved by paragraph 6 of Article 1 (General Scope).

Although the rules allow each of the Contracting States to apply their domestic anti-abuse rules, the foreign tax credit rules provided in paragraphs 2 and 4 of Article 24 (Relief from Double Taxation) ensure that the Contracting State applying an anti-abuse rule to a resident of the other Contracting State maintains only a residual right to tax. The primary right to tax remains with the country of residence. Accordingly, pursuant to subparagraph (b) of paragraph 2 of Article 24, if the gains subject to this rule are derived while the former U.K. resident was a resident of the United States, then such gains are considered to be gains from sources within the United States. Pursuant to paragraph 4 of Article 24, the United Kingdom will grant a foreign tax credit for U.S. tax imposed upon those gains.

Example. In year 1, U.K. resident A purchases stock in a Country X company for $1,000. A moves to the United States in year 2, when the fair market value of the stock is $2,000. In year 3, while A is still a U.S. resident, A sells the Country X stock. In year 4, after the sale of the Country X stock, A moves back to the United Kingdom and re-establishes residence. Under Article 13 (6), both the United States and the United Kingdom may tax the gain on the sale of the property in year 3. Under Article 24, however, the gain from the sale of the Country X stock is deemed to be from sources within the United States because A was a U.S. resident when the sale occurred and gains from the stock could be taxed by the United Kingdom only pursuant to paragraph 6 of Article 13 (that is, the stock could not be taxed under paragraph

1 or 3 of Article 13). Thus the United Kingdom is required to provide a foreign tax credit for U.S. taxes paid with respect to gain on the disposition of the Country X stock.

Relation to Other Articles

Notwithstanding the foregoing limitations on taxation of certain gains by the State of source, the saving clause of paragraph 4 of Article 1 (General Scope) permits the United States to tax its citizens and residents as if the Convention had not come into effect. Thus, any limitation in this Article on the right of the United States to tax gains does not apply to gains of a U.S. citizen or resident.

The benefits of this Article are also subject to the provisions of Article 23 (Limitation on Benefits). Thus, only a resident of a Contracting State that satisfies one of the conditions in Article 23 is entitled to the benefits of this Article.

Article 14 (Income from Employment)

Article 14 apportions taxing jurisdiction over remuneration derived by a resident of a Contracting State as an employee between the States of source and residence.

Paragraph 1

The general rule of Article 14 is contained in paragraph 1. Remuneration derived by a resident of a Contracting State as an employee may be taxed by the State of residence, and the remuneration also may be taxed by the other Contracting State to the extent derived from employment exercised (*i.e.*, services performed) in that other Contracting State. Paragraph 1 also provides that the more specific rules of Articles 15 (Directors' Fees), 17 (Pensions, Social Security, Annuities, Alimony and Child Support), and 19 (Government Service) apply in the case of employment income described in one of those articles. Thus, even though the State of source has a right to tax employment income under Article 14, it may not have the right to tax that income under the Convention if the income is described, for example, in Article 17 (Pensions, Social Security, Annuities, Alimony and Child Support) and is not taxable in the State of source under the provisions of that article.

The Convention refers to "salaries, wages and other similar remuneration," while the U.S. Model refers to "salaries, wages and other remuneration." The U.S. Model language was intended to make clear that Article 14 applies to any form of compensation, including payments in kind, regardless of whether the remuneration is "similar" to salaries or wages. The U.S. Model language is no longer necessary because of a recent addition to the Commentary to Article 16 of the OECD Model; paragraph 1.1 now confirms that payments in kind are covered by the Article.

Consistently with section 864(c)(6) of the Code, Article 14 also applies regardless of the timing of actual payment for services. Thus, a bonus paid to a resident of a Contracting State with respect to services performed in the other Contracting State with respect to a particular taxable year would be subject to Article 14 for that year even if it was paid after the close of the year. Similarly, an annuity received for services performed in a taxable year would be subject to

Article 14 despite the fact that it was paid in subsequent years. In either case, whether such payments were taxable in the State where the employment was exercised would depend on whether the tests of paragraph 2 were satisfied. Consequently, a person who receives the right to a future payment in consideration for services rendered in a Contracting State would be taxable in that State even if the payment is received at a time when the recipient is a resident of the other Contracting State.

The notes contain special rules regarding employee share or stock options. As a general matter, the notes clarify that any benefits, income or gains enjoyed by employees under share- or stock-option plans are regarded as "other similar remuneration" subject to Article 14. The notes also provide a specific rule for allocation of taxing rights where: (1) an employee has been granted a stock or share option in the course of employment in one of the Contracting States, (2) he has exercised that employment in both States during the period between grant and exercise of the option, (3) he remains in that employment at the date of the exercise, and (4), under the domestic law of the Contracting States, he would be taxable by both Contracting States in respect of the option gain. In this situation, each Contracting State may tax as State of source only that portion of the option gain which relates to the period or periods between the grant and the exercise of the option during which the individual has exercised the employment in that Contracting State. The portion attributable to a Contracting State will be determined by multiplying the gain by a fraction, the numerator of which is the number of days during which the employee exercised his employment in that State and the denominator of which will be the total number of days between grant and exercise of the option. The competent authorities of the Contracting States will endeavor to resolve by mutual agreement any difficulties or doubts arising as to the interpretation or application of Article 14 and Article 24 (Relief from Double Taxation) in relation to employee stock or share option plans.

Paragraph 2

Paragraph 2 sets forth an exception to the general rule that employment income may be taxed in the State where the employment is exercised. Under paragraph 2, the State where the employment is exercised may not tax the income from the employment if three conditions are satisfied: (1) the individual is present in the other Contracting State for a period or periods not exceeding 183 days in any 12-month period that begins or ends during the relevant (*i.e.*, the year in which the services are performed) calendar year; (2) the remuneration is paid by, or on behalf of, an employer who is not a resident of that other Contracting State; and (3) the remuneration is not borne by a permanent establishment that the employer has in that other State. In order for the remuneration to be exempt from tax in the source State, all three conditions must be satisfied. This exception is identical to that set forth in the U.S. and OECD Models.

The 183-day period in condition (a) is to be measured using the "days of physical presence" method. Under this method, the days that are counted include any day in which a part of the day is spent in the host country. *See* Rev. Rul. 56-24, 1956-1 C.B. 851. Thus, days that are counted include the days of arrival and departure; weekends and holidays on which the employee does not work but is present within the country; vacation days spent in the country before, during or after the employment period, unless the individual's presence before or after the employment can be shown to be independent of his presence there for employment purposes; and time during periods of sickness, training periods, strikes, etc., when the individual is present but not working. If illness prevented the individual from leaving the country in sufficient time to qualify for the benefit, those days will not count. Also, any part of a day spent in the host country while in transit between two points outside the host country is not counted. These rules are consistent with the description of the 183-day period in paragraph 5 of the Commentary to Article 15 in the OECD Model.

Conditions (b) and (c) are intended to ensure that a Contracting State will not be required to allow a deduction to the payer for compensation paid and at the same time to exempt the employee on the amount received. Accordingly, if a foreign person pays the salary of an employee who is employed in the host State, but a host State corporation or permanent establishment reimburses the payer with a payment that can be identified as a reimbursement, neither condition (b) nor (c), as the case may be, will be considered to have been fulfilled.

The reference to remuneration "borne by" a permanent establishment is understood to encompass all expenses that economically are incurred and not merely expenses that are currently deductible for tax purposes. Accordingly, the expenses referred to include expenses that are capitalizable as well as those that are currently deductible. Further, salaries paid by residents that are exempt from income taxation may be considered to be borne by a permanent establishment notwithstanding the fact that the expenses will be neither deductible nor capitalizable since the payer is exempt from tax.

Paragraph 3

Paragraph 3 contains a special rule applicable to remuneration for services performed by a resident of a Contracting State as an employee aboard a ship or aircraft operated in international traffic. Such remuneration may be taxed only in the State of residence of the employee if the services are performed as a member of the regular complement of the ship or aircraft. The "regular complement" includes the crew. In the case of a cruise ship, for example, it may also include others, such as entertainers, lecturers, etc., employed by the shipping company to serve on the ship throughout its voyage. The use of the term "regular complement" is intended to clarify that a person who exercises his employment as, for example, an insurance salesman while aboard a ship or aircraft is not covered by this paragraph.

Relation to other Articles

Notwithstanding the foregoing limitations on taxation of certain income by the State of source, the saving clause of paragraph 4 of Article 1 (General Scope) permits the United States to tax its citizens and residents as if the Convention had not come into effect. Thus, any limitation in this Article on the right of the United States to tax income from employment does not apply to income of a U.S. citizen or resident.

Article 15 (Directors' Fees)

This Article provides that a Contracting State may tax the fees and other compensation paid by a company that is a resident of that State for services performed in that State by a resident of the other Contracting State in his capacity as a director of the company. This rule is an exception to the more general rules of Articles 7 (Business Profits) and 14 (Income from Employment). Thus, for example, in determining whether a director's fee paid to a non-employee director is subject to tax in the country of residence of the company, it is not relevant to establish whether the fee is attributable to a permanent establishment in that State.

The analogous OECD provision reaches a different result in certain cases. Under the OECD Model provision, a resident of one Contracting State who is a director of a company that is resident in the other Contracting State is subject to tax in that other State in respect of his directors' fees regardless of where the services are performed. The United States has entered a reservation with respect to the OECD provision. Under this Convention, the State of residence of the company may tax nonresident directors with no time or dollar threshold, but only with respect to remuneration for services performed in that State.

The Convention refers to "similar payments," while the U.S. Model refers to "other compensation." The U.S. Model language was intended to make clear that Article 15 applies to any form of compensation, including payments in kind, regardless of whether the remuneration is "similar" to directors' fees. The U.S. Model language is no longer necessary because of a recent addition to the Commentary to Article 16 of the OECD Model; paragraph 1.1 now confirms that payments in kind are covered by the Article.

Article 15 is subject to the saving clause of paragraph 4 of Article 1 (General Scope). Thus, if a U.S. citizen who is a resident of the United Kingdom is a director of a U.S. corporation, the United States may tax his full remuneration regardless of where he performs his services.

Article 16 (Entertainers and Sportsmen)

This Article deals with the taxation in a Contracting State of entertainers and sportsmen resident in the other Contracting State from the performance of their services as such. The Article applies both to the income of an entertainer or sportsman who performs services on his own behalf and one who performs services on behalf of another person, either as an employee of that person, or pursuant to any other arrangement. The rules of this Article take precedence, in some circumstances, over those of Articles 7 (Business Profits) and 14 (Income from Employment).

This Article applies only with respect to the income of entertainers and sportsmen. Others involved in a performance or athletic event, such as producers, directors, technicians, managers, coaches, etc., remain subject to the provisions of Articles 7 and 14. In addition, except as provided in paragraph 2, income earned by juridical persons is not covered by Article 16.

Paragraph 1

Paragraph 1 describes the circumstances in which a Contracting State may tax the performance income of an entertainer or sportsman who is a resident of the other Contracting State. Under the paragraph, income derived by an individual resident of a Contracting State from activities as an entertainer or sportsman exercised in the other Contracting State may be taxed in that other State if the amount of the gross receipts derived by the performer exceeds $20,000 (or its equivalent in pounds sterling) for the taxable year. The $20,000 includes expenses reimbursed to the individual or borne on his behalf. If the gross receipts exceed $20,000, the full amount, not just the excess, may be taxed in the State of performance.

The OECD Model provides for taxation by the country of performance of the remuneration of entertainers or sportsmen with no dollar or time threshold. This Convention introduces the dollar threshold test to distinguish between two groups of entertainers and athletes -- those who are paid relatively large sums of money for very short periods of service, and who would, therefore, normally be exempt from host country tax under the standard personal services income rules, and those who earn relatively modest amounts and are, therefore, not easily distinguishable from those who earn other types of personal service income. The United States has entered a reservation to the OECD Model on this point.

Tax may be imposed under paragraph 1 even if the performer would have been exempt from tax under Article 7 (Business Profits) or 14 (Income from Employment). On the other hand. if the performer would be exempt from host-country tax under Article 16, but would be taxable under either Article 7 or 14, tax may be imposed under either of those Articles. Thus, for example, if a performer derives remuneration from his activities in an independent capacity, and the performer does not have a permanent establishment in the host State, he may be taxed by the host State in accordance with Article 16 if his remuneration exceeds $20,000 annually, despite the fact that he generally would be exempt from host State taxation under Article 7. However, a performer who receives less than the $20,000 threshold amount and therefore is not taxable under Article 17, nevertheless may be subject to tax in the host country under Article 7 or 14 if the tests for host-country taxability under the relevant Article are met. For example, if an entertainer who is an independent contractor earns $14,000 of income in a State for the calendar year, but the income is attributable to his permanent establishment in the State of performance, that State may tax his income under Article 7.

Since it frequently is not possible to know until year-end whether the income an entertainer or sportsman derived from performances in a Contracting State will exceed $20,000, nothing in the Convention precludes that Contracting State from withholding tax during the year and refunding it after the close of the year if the taxability threshold has not been met.

As explained in paragraph 9 of the Commentary to Article 17 of the OECD Model, Article 16 of the Convention applies to all income connected with a performance by the entertainer, such as appearance fees, award or prize money, and a share of the gate receipts. Income derived from a Contracting State by a performer who is a resident of the other Contracting State from other than actual performance, such as royalties from record sales and payments for product endorsements, is not covered by this Article, but by other articles of the Convention, such as Article 12 (Royalties) or Article 7 (Business Profits). For example, if an entertainer receives royalty income from the sale of live recordings, the royalty income would be exempt from source state tax under Article 12, even if the performance was conducted in the source country, although the entertainer could be taxed in the source country with respect to income from the performance itself under Article 16 if the dollar threshold is exceeded.

In determining whether income falls under Article 16 or another article, the controlling factor will be whether the income in question is predominantly attributable to the performance itself or to other activities or property rights. For instance, a fee paid to a performer for endorsement of a performance in which the performer will participate would be considered to be so closely associated with the performance itself that it normally would fall within Article 16. Similarly, a sponsorship fee paid by a business in return for the right to attach its name to the performance would be so closely associated with the performance that it would fall under Article 16 as well. As indicated in paragraph 9 of the Commentary to Article 17 of the OECD Model, however, a cancellation fee would not be considered to fall within Article 16 but would be dealt with under Article 7 (Business Profits) or 14 (Income from Employment).

As indicated in paragraph 4 of the Commentary to Article 17 of the OECD Model, where an individual fulfills a dual role as performer and non-performer (such as a player-coach or an actor-director), but his role in one of the two capacities is negligible, the predominant character of the individual's activities should control the characterization of those activities. In other cases there should be an apportionment between the performance-related compensation and other compensation.

Consistently with Article 14 (Income from Employment), Article 16 also applies regardless of the timing of actual payment for services. Thus, a bonus paid to a resident of a Contracting State with respect to a performance in the other Contracting State during a particular taxable year would be subject to Article 16 for that year even if it was paid after the close of the year.

Paragraph 2

Paragraph 2 is intended to deal with the potential for abuse when a performer's income does not accrue directly to the performer himself, but to another person. Foreign performers frequently perform in the United States as employees of, or under contract with, a company or other person.

The relationship may truly be one of employee and employer, with no abuse of the tax system either intended or realized. On the other hand, the "employer" may, for example, be a company established and owned by the performer, which is merely acting as the nominal income recipient in respect of the remuneration for the performance (a "star company"). The performer may act as an "employee," receive a modest salary, and arrange to receive the remainder of the income from his performance in another form or at a later time. In such case, absent the provisions of paragraph 2, the income arguably could escape host-country tax because the company earns business profits but has no permanent establishment in that country. The performer may largely or entirely escape host-country tax by receiving only a small salary in the year the services are performed, perhaps small enough to place him below the dollar threshold in paragraph 1. The performer might arrange to receive further payments in a later year, when he is not subject to host-country tax, perhaps as deferred salary payments, dividends or liquidating distributions.

Paragraph 2 seeks to prevent this type of abuse while at the same time protecting the taxpayers' rights to the benefits of the Convention when there is a legitimate employee-employer relationship between the performer and the person providing his services. Under paragraph 2, when the income accrues to a person other than the performer, and the performer or related persons participate, directly or indirectly, in the receipts or profits of that other person, the income may be taxed in the Contracting State where the performer's services are exercised, without regard to the provisions of the Convention concerning business profits (Article 7) or income from employment (Article 14). Thus, even if the "employer" has no permanent establishment in the host country, its income may be subject to tax there under the provisions of paragraph 2. Taxation under paragraph 2 is on the person providing the services of the performer. This paragraph does not affect the rules of paragraph 1, which apply to the performer himself. The income taxable by virtue of paragraph 2 is reduced to the extent of salary payments to the performer, which fall under paragraph 1.

For purposes of paragraph 2, income is deemed to accrue to another person (*i.e.*, the person providing the services of the performer) if that other person has control over, or the right to receive, gross income in respect of the services of the performer. Direct or indirect participation in the profits of a person may include, but is not limited to, the accrual or receipt of deferred remuneration, bonuses, fees, dividends, partnership income or other income or distributions.

Paragraph 2 does not apply if the person receiving the income establishes that neither the performer nor any persons related to the performer participate directly or indirectly in the receipts or profits of the person providing the services of the performer. Assume, for example, that a circus owned by a U.S. corporation performs in the United Kingdom, and promoters of the performance in the United Kingdom pay the circus, which, in turn, pays salaries to the circus performers. The circus is determined to have no permanent establishment in the United Kingdom. Since the circus performers do not participate in the profits of the circus, but merely receive their salaries out of the circus' gross receipts, the circus is protected by Article 7 and its income is not subject to host-country tax. Whether the salaries of the circus performers are subject to host-country tax under this Article depends on whether they exceed the $20,000 threshold in paragraph 1.

Since pursuant to Article 1 (General Scope) the Convention only applies to persons who are residents of one of the Contracting States, if the star company is not a resident of one of the Contracting States, then taxation of the income is not affected by Article 16 or any other provision of the Convention.

This exception from paragraph 2 for non-abusive cases is not found in the OECD Model. The United States has entered a reservation to the OECD Model on this point.

Relationship to other Articles

This Article is subject to the provisions of the saving clause of paragraph 4 of Article 1 (General Scope). Thus, if an entertainer or a sportsman who is resident in the United Kingdom is a citizen of the United States, the United States may tax all of his income from performances in the United States without regard to the provisions of this Article, subject, however, to the special foreign tax credit provisions of paragraph 6 of Article 24 (Relief from Double Taxation). In addition, benefits of this Article are subject to the provisions of Article 23 (Limitation on Benefits).

Article 17 (Pensions, Social Security, Annuities, Alimony, and Child Support)

This article deals with the taxation of private (*i.e.*, non-government service) pensions and annuities, social security benefits, alimony and child support payments.

Paragraph 1

Paragraph 1 provides as a general rule, in subparagraph (a), that the State of residence of the beneficial owner has the exclusive right to tax pensions and other similar remuneration. For this purpose, a payment is treated as a pension or other similar remuneration if it is a payment under a pension scheme, as defined in sub-paragraph (o) of paragraph 1 of Article 3 (General Definitions). While the term "pension" generally would include both periodic and lump-sum payments, paragraph 2 of the Article provides specific rules to deal with lump-sum payments, so they are not subject to the general rule of paragraph 1.

However, the State of residence, under subparagraph (b), must exempt from tax any amount of such pensions or other similar remuneration that would be exempt from tax in the State in which the pension scheme is established if the recipient were a resident of that State. Thus, for example, a distribution from a U.S. "Roth IRA" to a U.K. resident would be exempt from tax in the United Kingdom to the same extent the distribution would be exempt from tax in the United States if it were distributed to a U.S. resident. The same is true with respect to distributions from a traditional IRA to the extent that the distribution represents a return of non-deductible contributions. Similarly, if the distribution were not subject to tax when it was "rolled over" into another U.S. IRA (but not, for example, to a U.K. pension scheme), then the distribution would be exempt from tax in the United Kingdom.

Paragraph 2

Paragraph 2 is intended to deal with a particular type of double non-taxation that arose under the prior Convention because the United Kingdom does not tax lump-sum distributions from pension funds. Under the prior Convention, a lump-sum payment was treated in the same way as any other pension, and was taxable only in the country of residence of the beneficial owner. Accordingly, a person who anticipated receiving a lump-sum distribution from a U.S. pension scheme with respect to employment in the United States could avoid U.S. withholding tax on the distribution by establishing residence in the United Kingdom for the year in which he received the distribution. The person would not be subject to tax in either the United States or the United Kingdom with respect to the lump-sum distribution, resulting in a significant windfall.

Paragraph 2 prevents this unanticipated benefit by providing that, notwithstanding the exclusive residence-country taxation of paragraph 1, any lump-sum payment derived by a resident of a Contracting State from a pension scheme established in the other Contracting State shall be taxable in that other State.

Paragraph 3

Paragraph 3 provides for exclusive residence-country taxation of social security benefits. Like the prior Convention, but unlike the U.S. Model, the Convention provides that payments made by one of the Contracting States under the provisions of its social security or similar legislation to a resident of the other Contracting State will be taxable only in the other Contracting State. This paragraph applies to social security beneficiaries, whether they have contributed to the system as private-sector or government employees. The phrase "similar legislation" is intended to refer to United States Tier 1 Railroad Retirement benefits.

Paragraph 4

Under paragraph 4, any annuity that is derived and beneficially owned by an annuitant who is a resident of a Contracting State is taxable only in that State. The term "annuity" means a stated sum paid periodically at stated times during the life of the annuitant, or during a specified or ascertainable period of time, under an obligation to make the payments in return for adequate and full consideration (other than in return for services rendered). The term "annuity" does not include any distributions from a pension scheme that are described in paragraph 1. An annuity received in consideration for services rendered would be treated as deferred compensation and generally taxable in accordance with Article 7 (Business Profits) or Article 14 (Income from Employment), not Article 17.

Paragraph 5

Paragraph 5 generally covers periodic payments made pursuant to a written separation agreement or a decree of divorce, separate maintenance, or compulsory support. Paragraph 5 exempts from tax in both Contracting States such payments made by a resident of one of the Contracting States to a resident of the other Contracting State, unless the payments are deductible in the payer's State of residence. Thus, child support payments from a resident of a Contracting State to a resident of the other Contracting State are taxable in neither Contracting State, assuming that the payments are not deductible to the payer. By contrast, deductible alimony payments made by a resident of a Contracting State to a resident of the other Contracting State are taxable, exclusively, in the recipient's State of residence. Although the structure of the Article is different, the results are the same as under the U.S Model provisions.

Relation to other Articles

Subparagraph 1(a) is subject to the saving clause of paragraph 4 of Article 1 (General Scope) while subparagraph 1(b) is not, by reason of the exception in subparagraph 5(a) of Article 1. Thus, a U.S. citizen who is a resident of the United Kingdom and receives a pension will be subject to U.S. tax on the payment, notwithstanding the rules in those paragraphs that give the State of residence of the recipient the exclusive taxing right. However, a U.S. citizen who receives a distribution from a pension scheme established in the United Kingdom will be taxable on only the portion of the pension distribution that is taxable in the United Kingdom.

Paragraphs 2 and 4 of Article 17 also are subject to the saving clause. Accordingly, a U.S. citizen who is a resident of the United Kingdom will be subject to U.S. tax on a lump-sum distribution from a pension scheme or an annuity, notwithstanding the rules in those paragraphs that give exclusive taxation rights to the State of source or residence, as the case may be. Paragraphs 3 and 5 are exceptions to the saving clause. Accordingly, a U.S. citizen who is a resident of the United Kingdom will not be subject to U.S. tax on any U.S. social security benefits, child support payments or alimony.

Article 18 (Pension Schemes)

Article 18 deals with cross-border pension contributions. It is intended to remove barriers to the flow of personal services between the Contracting States that could otherwise result from discontinuities in the laws of the Contracting States regarding the deductibility of pension contributions. Such discontinuities may arise where countries allow deductions or exclusions to their residents for contributions, made by them or on their behalf, to resident pension plans, but do not allow deductions or exclusions for payments made to plans resident in another country, even if the structure and legal requirements of such plans in the two countries are similar.

There is no comparable set of rules in the OECD Model, although the issue is discussed in detail in the Commentary to Article 18 (Pensions). The U.S. Model deals with this issue in paragraph 6 of Article 18 (Pensions, Social Security, Annuities, Alimony and Child Support).

Paragraph 1

Paragraph 1 provides that if a resident of a Contracting State participates in a pension scheme established in the other Contracting State, the State of residence will not tax the income of the pension scheme with respect to that resident until a distribution is made from the pension scheme. Thus, for example, if a U.S. citizen contributes to a U.S. qualified plan while working in the United States and then establishes residence in the United Kingdom, paragraph 1 prevents the United Kingdom from taxing currently the plan's earnings and accretions with respect to that individual. When the resident receives a distribution from the pension scheme, that distribution may be subject to tax in the State of residence, subject to paragraphs 1 and 2 of Article 17 (Pensions, Social Security, Annuities, Alimony, and Child Support).

Paragraph 2

Paragraph 2 provides certain benefits with respect to cross-border contributions to a pension scheme, subject to the limitations of paragraphs 3 and 4 of the Article. It is irrelevant for purposes of paragraph 2 whether the participant establishes residence in the State where the individual renders services (the "host State"). The benefits provided in paragraph 2 are similar to the benefits the U.S. Model provides with respect to contributions.

Subparagraph (a) of paragraph 2 allows an individual who exercises employment or self-employment in a Contracting State to deduct or exclude from income in that Contracting State contributions made by or on behalf of the individual during the period of employment or self-employment to a pension scheme established in the other Contracting State. Thus, for example, if a participant in a U.S. qualified plan goes to work in the United Kingdom, the participant may deduct or exclude from income in the United Kingdom contributions to the U.S. qualified plan made while the participant works in the United Kingdom. Subparagraph (a), however, applies only to the extent of the relief allowed by the host State (*e.g.*, the United Kingdom in the example) for contributions to a pension scheme established in that State.

Subparagraph (b) of paragraph 2 provides that, in the case of employment, accrued benefits and contributions by or on behalf of the individual's employer, during the period of employment in the host State, will not be treated as taxable income to the employee in that State. Subparagraph (b) also allows the employer a deduction in computing business profits in the host State for contributions to the plan. For example, if a participant in a U.S. qualified plan goes to work in the United Kingdom, the participant's employer may deduct from its business profits in the United Kingdom contributions to the U.S. qualified plan for the benefit of the employee while the employee renders services in the United Kingdom.

As in the case of subparagraph (a), subparagraph (b) applies only to the extent of the relief allowed by the host State for contributions to pension schemes established in that State. Therefore, where the United States is the host State, the exclusion of employee contributions from the employee's income under this paragraph is limited to elective contributions not in excess of the amount specified in section 402(g). Deduction of employer contributions is subject to the limitations of sections 415 and 404. The section 404 limitation on deductions is calculated as if the individual were the only employee covered by the plan.

Paragraph 3

Paragraph 3 limits the availability of benefits under paragraph 2. Under subparagraph (a) of paragraph 3, paragraph 2 does not apply to contributions to a pension scheme unless the participant already was contributing to the scheme, or his employer already was contributing to the scheme with respect to that individual, before the individual began exercising employment in the State where the services are performed (the "host State"). This condition would be met if either the employee or the employer was contributing to a scheme that was replaced by the scheme to which he is contributing. The rule regarding successor schemes would apply if, for example, the employer has been taken over by a company that replaces the existing scheme with its own scheme, rolling membership in the old scheme over into the new scheme.

In addition, under subparagraph (b) of paragraph 3, the competent authority of the host State must determine that the recognized plan to which a contribution is made in the other Contracting State generally corresponds to the plan in the host State. According to the notes, it is understood for this purpose that U.S. pension schemes eligible for the benefits of paragraph 2 include qualified plans under section 401(a), individual retirement plans (including individual retirement plans that are part of a simplified employee pension plan that satisfies section 408(k)), individual retirement accounts, individual retirement annuities, section 408(p) accounts and Roth IRAs under section 408A), section 403(a) qualified annuity plans, and section 403(b) plans.

Paragraph 4

Paragraph 4 limits the availability of benefits under paragraph 2 of this article. Paragraph 4 provides a special rule in cases where income dealt with by the Convention is taxable to a resident of a Contracting State only if and to the extent it is remitted to or received by that person. In such cases, paragraph 4 reduces proportionately the deduction or exclusion of contributions to a pension scheme under subparagraph (a) of paragraph 2 based upon the amount of income subject to tax in the State of residence. Although this rule is written in bilateral fashion, it presently applies to residents of the United Kingdom only, because the United States does not tax on a remittance basis. Paragraph 4 would apply, for example, if a U.S. citizen resident in the United Kingdom earns income in the United States that is not subject to tax in the United Kingdom because the income is not remitted to the United Kingdom. In this case, paragraph 4 would reduce proportionately the amount of any deduction or exclusion allowed in the United Kingdom to the U.S. citizen by subparagraph (a) of paragraph 2 for contributions to a U.S. pension scheme.

Paragraph 5

Paragraph 5 generally provides U.S. tax treatment for certain contributions by or on behalf of U.S. citizens resident in the United Kingdom to pension schemes established in the United Kingdom that is comparable to the treatment that would be provided for contributions to U.S. schemes. Under subparagraph (a) of paragraph 5, a U.S. citizen resident in the United Kingdom may exclude or deduct for U.S. tax purposes certain contributions to a pension scheme established in the United Kingdom. Qualifying contributions generally include contributions made during the period the U.S. citizen exercises an employment in the United Kingdom if expenses of the employment are borne by a U.K. employer or U.K. permanent establishment. Similarly, with respect to the U.S. citizen's participation in the U.K. pension scheme, accrued benefits and contributions during that period generally are not treated as taxable income in the United States.

The U.S. tax benefit allowed by paragraph 5, however, is limited to the lesser of the amount of relief allowed for contributions and benefits under a pension scheme established in the United Kingdom and, under subparagraph (b), the amount of relief that would be allowed for contributions and benefits under a generally corresponding pension scheme established in the United States.

Subparagraph (c) provides that the benefits an individual obtains under paragraph 5 are counted when determining that individual's eligibility for benefits under a pension scheme established in the United States. Thus, for example, contributions to a U.K. pension scheme may be counted in determining whether the individual has exceeded the annual limitation on contributions to an individual retirement account.

Under subparagraph (d), paragraph 5 does not apply to pension contributions and benefits unless the competent authority of the United States has agreed that the pension scheme established in the United Kingdom generally corresponds to a pension scheme established in the United States. The notes provide that certain pension schemes have been determined to "generally correspond" to schemes in the other country. Since paragraph 5 applies only with respect to persons employed by a U.K. employer or U.K. permanent establishment, however, the relevant U.K. plans are those that correspond to employer plans in the United States. Accordingly, it applies with respect to retirement benefit schemes for the purpose of Chapter I of Part XIV of the Income and Corporation Taxes Act 1988.

Relation to other Articles

Paragraph 1 is not subject to the saving clause of paragraph 4 of Article 1 (General Scope) by reason of the exception in subparagraph 5(a) of Article 1. Accordingly, a U.S. citizen who is a resident of the United Kingdom will not be subject to tax in the United States on the earnings and accretions of a U.K. pension fund with respect to that U.S. citizen. Paragraph 2 is not subject to the saving clause by reason of subparagraph 5(b) of Article 1. Accordingly, the benefits of paragraph 2 will be available to residents of the United States who are not citizens of the United States nor admitted for permanent resident ("green card" holders) in the United States. Paragraph 5 is not subject to the saving clause of paragraph 4 of Article 1 by reason of the exception in subparagraph 5(a) of Article 1. Accordingly, U.S. citizens who are resident in the United Kingdom will receive the benefits provided by paragraph 5 with respect to contributions made to pension schemes established in the United Kingdom.

Article 19 (Government Service)

Paragraph 1

Subparagraphs (a) and (b) of paragraph 1 deal with the taxation of government compensation (other than a pension addressed in paragraph 2). Subparagraph (a) provides that remuneration paid from the public funds of one of the States or its political subdivisions or local authorities to any individual who is rendering services to that State, political subdivision or local authority is exempt from tax by the other State (the "host State"). Under subparagraph (b), such payments are, however, taxable exclusively in the other State (*i.e.*, the host State) if the services are rendered in that other State and the individual is a resident of that State who is either a national of that State or a person who did not become resident of that State solely for purposes of rendering the services.

This paragraph follows the OECD Model, but differs from the U.S. Model in applying only to government employees and not to independent contractors engaged by governments to perform services for them.

The remuneration described in paragraph 1 is subject to the provisions of this paragraph and not to those of Articles 14 (Income from Employment), 15 (Directors' Fees) or 16 (Entertainers and Sportsmen). If, however, the recipient of the income is employed by a business conducted by a local government, paragraph 3 provides that those other Articles will apply.

Paragraph 2

Paragraph 2 deals with the taxation of pensions paid by, or out of funds created by, one of the States, or a political subdivision or a local authority thereof, to an individual in respect of services rendered to that State or subdivision or authority. Subparagraph (a) provides that such pensions are taxable only in that State. Subparagraph (b) provides an exception under which such pensions are taxable only in the other State if the individual is a resident of, and a national of, that other State.

Pensions paid to retired civilian and military employees of a Government of either State are intended to be covered under paragraph 2. When benefits paid by a State in respect of services rendered to that State or a subdivision or authority are in the form of social security benefits, however, those payments are covered by paragraph 2 of Article 17 (Pensions, Social Security, Annuities, Alimony, and Child Support). The result will differ depending upon whether Article 17 or 19 applies, since social security benefits are generally taxable exclusively by the residence country while government pensions are generally taxable exclusively by the source country. The result will be the same only when the payment is made to a resident and national of the other Contracting State. In such a case, government pensions, like social security payments, are taxable only in the residence country.

Paragraph 3

Paragraph 3 specifies that paragraphs 1 and 2 do not apply to remuneration and pensions paid for services performed in connection with a business carried on by a Contracting State or a political subdivision of local authority thereof. In such cases, the remuneration and pensions are subjected instead to the provisions of Articles 14 (Income from Employment), 15 (Directors' Fees), 16 (Entertainers and Sportsmen) and 17 (Pensions, Social Security, Annuities, Alimony, and Child Support). This provision conforms to the OECD Model.

Relation to other Articles

Under paragraph 5(b) of Article 1 (General Scope), the saving clause (paragraph 4 of Article 1) does not apply to the benefits conferred by one of the States under Article 19 if the recipient of the benefits is neither a citizen of that State, nor a person who has been admitted for permanent residence there (*i.e.*, in the United States, a "green card" holder). Thus, for example, a resident of the United Kingdom who, in the course of rendering services to the government of the United Kingdom becomes a resident of the United States (but not a permanent resident), would be entitled to the exemption from source State taxation provided by paragraph 1. In addition, an individual who receives a pension paid by the Government of the United Kingdom in respect of services rendered to that Government is taxable on that pension only in the United Kingdom unless the individual is a U.S. citizen or acquires a U.S. green card.

Article 20 (Students)

Article 20 provides rules regarding the taxation of students and business apprentices. Persons who meet the tests of the article will be exempt from tax with respect to designated classes of income in the State they are visiting (the "host State"). Several conditions must be satisfied for an individual to be entitled to the benefits of this article.

First, the visitor must have been, either at the time of his arrival in the host State or immediately before, a resident of the other Contracting State.

Second, the purpose of the visit must be the full-time education or training of the visitor. Thus, if the visitor comes principally to work in the host State but also is a part-time student, he is not entitled to the benefits of this article, even with respect to any payments he may receive from abroad for his maintenance or education, and regardless of whether or not he is in a degree program. Whether a student is to be considered full-time will be determined by the rules of the educational institution where he is studying. A person who visits the host State to obtain business training and who also receives a salary from his employer for providing services would not be entitled to the benefits of this article with respect to the payments for services.

Third, a student must be studying at a university, college, or other recognized educational institution of a similar nature. The phrase "university, college, or other recognized educational institution of a similar nature" clarifies that a qualifying educational institution is one that offers a diversified curriculum for full-time students. An educational institution further is understood to be an institution that normally maintains a regular faculty and normally has a regular body of students in attendance at the place where the educational activities are carried on. An educational institution will be considered to be recognized if it is accredited by an authority that generally is responsible for accreditation of institutions in the particular field of study. This requirement does not apply to business trainees or apprentices.

The host-country exemption in Article 20 applies only to payments arising outside the host State that are received by the student, apprentice or business trainee for the purpose of his maintenance, education or training. A payment will be considered to arise outside the host State if the payer is located outside the host State. Thus, if an employer from one of the Contracting States sends an employee to the other Contracting State for training, the payments the trainee receives from abroad from his employer for his maintenance or training while he is present in the host State will be exempt from tax in the host State. Where appropriate, substance prevails over form in determining the identity of the payer. Thus, for example, payments made directly or indirectly by a U.S. person with whom the visitor is training, but which have been routed through a source outside the United States (*e.g.*, a foreign bank account), are not treated as arising outside the United States for this purpose.

In the case of an apprentice or business trainee, the benefits of this article will extend only for a period of one year from the time that the visitor first arrives in the host State. If, however, an apprentice or trainee remains in the host State for a second year, thus losing the benefits of the article, he does not retroactively lose the benefits of the article for the first year.

The saving clause of paragraph 4 of Article 1 (General Scope) does not apply to this article with respect to an individual who is neither a citizen of the host State nor has been admitted for permanent residence there. The saving clause, however, does apply with respect to citizens and permanent residents of the host State. Accordingly, a U.S. citizen who is a resident of the United Kingdom and who visits the United States as a full-time student at an accredited university will not be exempt from U.S. tax on remittances from abroad that otherwise constitute U.S. taxable income. Under subparagraph (b) of paragraph 5 of Article 1, however, a U.K. resident who is not a U.S. citizen, and who visits the United States as a student and remains long enough to become a resident under U.S. law, but does not become a permanent resident (*i.e.*, does not acquire a green card), will be entitled to the full benefits of the article.

Article 20A (Teachers)

Paragraph 1

Paragraph 1 of Article 20A provides that a professor or teacher who visits one of the Contracting States for a period not exceeding two years, for the purpose of teaching or engaging in research at a university, college, or other recognized educational institution in that Contracting State, and who is immediately before that visit a resident of the other Contracting State, will be exempted from tax by the first-mentioned Contracting State on any remuneration for such teaching or research for a period not exceeding two years from the date he first visits that State for the purpose of teaching or engaging in research. Since this two year period is determined from the date he first visits the Contracting State, periodic vacations outside the first-mentioned Contracting State, or a brief return to the other Contracting State will not toll the running of the two year period. Like the existing Convention, if the two-year period beginning from the date of his arrival is exceeded, the exemption will be lost retroactively. Thus, if a person comes to a Contracting State for the purpose of teaching and stays for a period in excess of two years, the exemption will not apply for the first two years.

A person who meets the qualifications for this exemption may again claim its benefits if he first re-establishes his residence in the other Contracting State. In such case, the person claiming these benefits on a subsequent occasion must first satisfy the competent authority of the first-mentioned Contracting State that he had become a resident of the other State for a substantial period of time (normally at least one year).

Paragraph 2

Under paragraph 2, the Contracting State in which the teaching or research is performed may apply this exemption either to current payments to a professor or teacher in anticipation of fulfillment of the requirements of paragraph 1 or by way of withholding and refund. Thus, the recipient may be required to report and pay taxes on such income on a current basis and seek a refund of taxes paid upon fulfillment of the requirements of paragraph 1.

Paragraph 3

Pursuant to paragraph 3, this Article only applies to income from research undertaken in the public interest which is not primarily for the benefit of a private person or persons. For example, research projects which are undertaken to discover or perfect product processes, designs, etc., which are expected to be commercially exploited by the researcher or his present (or former) employer do not qualify under this Article.

Relation to other Articles

The saving clause of paragraph 4 of Article 1 (General Scope) does not apply to this article with respect to an individual who is neither a citizen of the host State nor has been admitted for permanent residence there. The saving clause, however, does apply with respect to citizens and permanent residents of the host State. Accordingly, a U.S. citizen who is a resident of the United Kingdom and who visits the United States to teach at a university will not be exempt from U.S. tax on his salary. Under subparagraph (b) of paragraph 5 of Article 1, however, a person who is not a U.S. citizen, and who visits the United States as a teacher and remains long enough to become a resident under U.S. law, but does not become a permanent resident (*i.e.*, does not acquire a green card), will be entitled to the full benefits of the article.

Article 21 (Offshore Exploration and Exploitation Activities)

This article deals exclusively with the taxation of activities carried on by a resident of one of the Contracting States on the continental shelf of the other Contracting State in connection with the exploration or exploitation of the natural resources of the shelf, principally activities connected with exploration for oil by offshore drilling rigs. In the U.S. and OECD Models, the income from these activities is subject to the standard rules found in the other articles of the Models (*e.g.*, the business profits and personal services articles). In the Convention, this Article overrides Article 7 (Business Profits) to the extent this Article is inconsistent with Article 7. The provision carries over, with some modifications, from the prior Convention.

Paragraph 1

Paragraph 1 states that the provisions of this article apply, notwithstanding any other provision of the Convention, to activities carried on offshore in a Contracting State in connection with the exploration or exploitation of the sea bed and subsoil and their natural resources situated in that State. These activities are referred to as "exploration activities" and "exploitation activities" and include, but are not limited to, the exploration for and extraction of oil, minerals, and natural gas.

Although there are no explicit references to other articles, the implicit references are principally to Articles 5 (Permanent Establishment), 7 (Business Profits), and 14 (Income from Employment). For example, if a drilling rig of a U.S. enterprise is present on the continental shelf of the United Kingdom for 10 months and would, therefore, not give rise to a permanent establishment because of the 12-month construction site rule of paragraph 3 of Article 5, the rig would, nevertheless, be deemed to create a permanent establishment under paragraph 2 of Article 21.

Paragraph 2

Paragraphs 2 and 3 provide the basic rules for determining when an enterprise is deemed to have a permanent establishment as a result of offshore activities. The general rule is that all exploitation activities give rise to a permanent establishment, while exploration activities create a permanent establishment only if they continue for a period exceeding, in the aggregate, 30 days in a twelve-month period. Accordingly, paragraph 2 provides that, subject to the exception of paragraph 3, an enterprise of one Contracting State carrying on exploration activities or exploitation activities in the other Contracting State will be deemed to be carrying on business through a permanent establishment situated therein.

Paragraph 3

Paragraph 3 provides that an enterprise of a Contracting State carrying on exploration activities in the other Contracting State will not create a permanent establishment therein unless the activities are carried on there for a period or periods aggregating more than 30 days within any period of twelve months. This 30-day time period carries over from the prior Convention.

Paragraph 3 also provides rules for aggregating the activities of related parties for purposes of determining whether the 30-day threshold has been exceeded. If the enterprise carrying on the offshore activities is associated with another enterprise, and that associated enterprise also is carrying on substantially similar exploration activities in the host State, the former enterprise shall be deemed to be carrying on all such activities. The aggregation rule is intended to prevent taxpayers from avoiding the time threshold by artificially splitting activities between different entities. Thus, the rule will not apply to the extent that the activities of the two persons are being carried on at the same time. For purposes of paragraph 3, an enterprise is associated with another if one participates directly or indirectly in the management, control or capital of the other or if the same persons participate directly or indirectly in the management, control or capital of both enterprises.

Paragraph 4

Paragraph 4 provides thresholds for the taxation of income from employment in respect of offshore activities. As a general rule, the Contracting State where the activities are carried on (the "host State") may tax salaries, wages, and other similar remuneration derived by an individual who is a resident of the other State in respect of employment exercised in connection with the offshore activities described in the preceding paragraphs of this article, to the extent that the duties are performed offshore in the host State.

If, however, such employment is carried on for a period or periods aggregating 30 days or less in any 12-month period, only the State of residence of the employee, and not the host State, may tax the income of the employee in respect of such employment. This provision may in certain circumstances give rise to a taxing right in the host State that would not exist in the absence of this Article.

Relation to other Articles

This Article is subject to the saving clause of paragraph 4 of Article 1 (General Scope). Thus, the United States may tax the income of a resident of the United Kingdom who is a U.S. citizen even if, under the provisions of this Article, a resident of the United Kingdom would not be subject to U.S. tax. As with any benefit of the Convention, a person claiming a benefit under this Article must be entitled to the benefit under the provisions of Article 23 (Limitation on Benefits).

Article 22 (Other Income)

Article 22 generally assigns taxing jurisdiction over income not dealt with in the other articles (Articles 6 through 21) of the Convention to the State of residence of the beneficial owner of the income. An item of income is "dealt with" in another article if it is the type of income described in the article and it has its source in a Contracting State. For example, all royalty income that arises in a Contracting State and that is beneficially owned by a resident of the other Contracting State is "dealt with" in Article 12 (Royalties).

Examples of items of income covered by Article 22 include income from gambling, punitive (but not compensatory) damages, covenants not to compete, and income from certain financial instruments to the extent derived by persons not engaged in the trade or business of dealing in such instruments (unless the transaction giving rise to the income is related to a trade or business, in which case it is dealt with under Article 7 (Business Profits)). The article also applies to items of income that are not dealt with in the other articles because of their source or some other characteristic. For example, Article 11 (Interest) addresses only the taxation of interest arising in a Contracting State. Interest arising in a third State that is not attributable to a permanent establishment, therefore, is subject to Article 22.

Distributions from partnerships are not generally dealt with under Article 22 because partnership distributions generally do not constitute income. Under the Code, partners include in income their distributive share of partnership income annually, and partnership distributions themselves generally do not give rise to income. This would also be the case under U.S. law with respect to distributions from trusts. Under the Code, trust income and distributions have the character of the associated distributable net income and therefore would generally be covered by another article of the Convention. See Code section 641 et seq. The Convention provides a specific carve-out with respect to income paid out of trusts or the estates of deceased persons in order to provide the same result in the United Kingdom as would apply under U.S. domestic law. The notes confirm that distributions from trusts or the estates of deceased persons will be characterized according to the character of the underlying income.

Paragraph 1

The general rule of Article 22 is contained in paragraph 1. Items of income not dealt with in other articles and beneficially owned by a resident of a Contracting State will be taxable only in the State of residence. This exclusive right of taxation applies whether or not the residence State exercises its right to tax the income covered by the Article.

The reference in this paragraph to "items of income beneficially owned by a resident of a Contracting State" rather than simply "items of income of a resident of a Contracting State," as in the OECD Model, is intended merely to make explicit the implicit understanding in other treaties that the exclusive residence taxation provided by paragraph 1 applies only when a resident of a Contracting State is the beneficial owner of the income. Thus, source taxation of income not dealt with in other articles of the Convention is not limited by paragraph 1 if it is nominally paid to a resident of the other Contracting State, but is beneficially owned by a resident of a third State. However, income received by a nominee on behalf of a resident of that other State would be entitled to benefits.

The term "beneficially owned" is not defined in the Convention, and is, therefore, defined as under the internal law of the country imposing tax (*i.e.*, the source country). The person who beneficially owns the income for purposes of Article 22 is the person to which the income is attributable for tax purposes under the laws of the source State.

Paragraph 2

This paragraph provides an exception to the general rule of paragraph 1 for income, other than income from real property, that is attributable to a permanent establishment maintained in a Contracting State by a resident of the other Contracting State. The taxation of such income is governed by the provisions of Article 7 (Business Profits). Therefore, income arising outside the United States that is attributable to a permanent establishment maintained in the United States by a resident of the United Kingdom generally would be taxable by the United States under the provisions of Article 7. This would be true even if the income is sourced in a third State.

Paragraph 3

Paragraph 3 is not found in the U.S. or OECD Models, but is suggested in the Commentary to Article 21 of the OECD Model. The paragraph restricts the operation of Article 22 where, by reason of a special relationship between the payer and the beneficial owner or between both of them and some other person, the amount of other income paid exceeds the amount which would have been agreed upon by the parties had they stipulated at arm's length. This rule applies, for example, to payments pursuant to non-traditional financial instruments, such as equity swaps. Article 22 applies in such a case only to the arm's-length amount, and the excess part of the payment remains taxable according to the laws of the two Contracting States, due regard being had to the other provisions of the Convention.

Paragraph 4

Paragraph 4 provides that Article 22 will not apply to any income paid under, or as part of, a conduit arrangement. The term "conduit arrangement" is defined in subparagraph (n) of paragraph 1 of Article 3 (General Definitions). As discussed in the Technical Explanation to that provision, the United States will interpret this rule co-extensively and consistently with U.S. domestic law, including in particular the rules of regulation section 1.881-3 and other regulations adopted under the authority of section 7701(l) of the Code.

Relation to Other Articles

This Article is subject to the saving clause of paragraph 4 of Article 1 (General Scope). Thus, the United States may tax the income of a resident of the United Kingdom that is not dealt with elsewhere in the Convention, if that resident is a citizen of the United States.

The benefits of this Article are also subject to the provisions of Article 23 (Limitation on Benefits). Thus, only a resident of a Contracting State that satisfies one of the conditions in Article 23 is entitled to the benefits of this Article.

Article 23 (Limitation on Benefits)

Purpose of Limitation on Benefits Provisions

The United States views an income tax treaty as a vehicle for providing treaty benefits to residents of the two Contracting States. This statement begs the question of who is to be treated as a resident of a Contracting State for the purpose of being granted treaty benefits. The Commentaries to the OECD Model authorize a tax authority to deny benefits, under substance-over-form principles, to a nominee in one State deriving income from the other on behalf of a third-country resident. In addition, although the text of the OECD Model does not contain express anti-abuse provisions, the Commentary to Article 1 contains an extensive discussion approving the use of such provisions in tax treaties in order to limit the ability of third state residents to obtain treaty benefits. The United States holds strongly to the view that tax treaties should include provisions that specifically prevent misuse of treaties by residents of third countries. Consequently, all recent U.S. income tax treaties contain comprehensive Limitation on Benefits provisions.

A treaty that provides treaty benefits to any resident of a Contracting State permits "treaty shopping": the use, by residents of third states, of legal entities established in a Contracting State with a principal purpose to obtain the benefits of a tax treaty between the United States and the other Contracting State. It is important to note that this definition of treaty shopping does not encompass every case in which a third state resident establishes an entity in a U.S. treaty partner, and that entity enjoys treaty benefits to which the third state resident would not itself be entitled. If the third country resident had substantial reasons for establishing the structure that were unrelated to obtaining treaty benefits, the structure would not fall within the definition of treaty shopping set forth above.

Of course, the fundamental problem presented by this approach is that it is based on the taxpayer's motives in establishing an entity in a particular country, which a tax administrator is normally ill-equipped to identify. In order to avoid the necessity of making this subjective determination, Article 23 sets forth a series of objective tests. The assumption underlying each of these tests is that a taxpayer that satisfies the requirements of the test probably has a real business purpose for the structure it has adopted, or has a sufficiently strong nexus to the other Contracting State (*e.g.*, a resident individual) to warrant benefits even in the absence of a business connection, and that this business purpose or connection is sufficient to justify the conclusion that obtaining the benefits of the treaty is not a principal purpose of establishing or maintaining residence in that other State.

For instance, the assumption underlying the active trade or business test under paragraph 4 is that a third country resident that establishes a "substantial" operation in the United Kingdom and that derives income from a similar activity in the United States would not do so primarily to avail itself of the benefits of the Convention; it is presumed in such a case that the investor had a valid business purpose for investing in the United Kingdom, and that the link between that trade or business and the U.S. activity that generates the treaty-benefited income manifests a business purpose for placing the U.S. investments in the entity in the United Kingdom. It is considered unlikely that the investor would incur the expense of establishing a substantial trade or business in the United Kingdom simply to obtain the benefits of the Convention. A similar rationale underlies other tests in Article 23.

While these tests provide useful surrogates for identifying actual intent, these mechanical tests cannot account for every case in which the taxpayer was not treaty shopping. Accordingly, Article 23 also includes a provision (paragraph 6) authorizing the competent authority of a Contracting State to grant benefits. While an analysis under paragraph 6 may well differ from that under one of the other tests of Article 23, its objective is the same: to identify investors whose residence in the other State can be justified by factors other than a purpose to derive treaty benefits.

Article 23 and the anti-abuse provisions of domestic law complement each other, as Article 23 effectively determines whether an entity has a sufficient nexus to the Contracting State to be treated as a resident for treaty purposes, while domestic anti-abuse provisions (*e.g.*, business purpose, substance-over-form, step transaction or conduit principles) determine whether a particular transaction should be recast in accordance with its substance. Thus, internal law principles of the source State may be applied to identify the beneficial owner of an item of income, and Article 23 then will be applied to the beneficial owner to determine if that person is entitled to the benefits of the Convention with respect to such income.

Each of the substantive provisions of Article 23 states that benefits shall be granted only if the resident of a Contracting State satisfies any other specified conditions for claiming benefits. This means, for example, that a publicly-traded company that satisfies the conditions of subparagraph 2(c) will be eligible for the exemption from withholding tax on dividends at source only if it also satisfies the 12-month holding period requirement of subparagraph 3(a) of Article 10 (Dividends). Moreover, a company that is eligible for benefits with respect to dividend income pursuant to either paragraph 4 of Article 23 or subparagraph (d) or (f) of paragraph 2 will not be eligible for the withholding tax exemption of subparagraph 3(a) of Article 10 unless it also satisfies the October 1, 1998 requirement of clause (i) of subparagraph 3(a).

Article 23 (Limitation on Benefits)

Article 23 follows the form used in other recent U.S. income tax treaties. Paragraph 1 states the general rule that a resident of a Contracting State is entitled to benefits otherwise accorded to residents only to the extent that the resident satisfies the requirements of the Article and any other specified conditions for the obtaining of such benefits. Paragraph 2 lists a series of attributes of a resident of a Contracting State, any one of which suffices to make such resident a "qualified person" and thus entitled to all the benefits of the Convention. Paragraph 3 provides a so-called "derivative benefits" test under which certain categories of income may qualify for benefits. Paragraph 4 sets forth the active trade or business test, under which a person not entitled to benefits under paragraph 2 may nonetheless be granted benefits with regard to certain types of income. Paragraph 5 limits the benefits available under the other provisions of the Article in certain cases involving the issuance of "tracking stock" and similar instruments. Paragraph 6 provides that benefits may also be granted if the competent authority of the State from which the benefits are claimed determines that it is appropriate to grant benefits in that case. Paragraph 7 defines the terms used specifically in this Article.

Paragraph 1

Paragraph 1 provides that, except as otherwise provided, a resident of a Contracting State will be entitled to all the benefits of the Convention otherwise accorded to residents of a Contracting State only if the resident is a "qualified person" as defined in paragraph 2 of Article 23.

The benefits otherwise accorded to residents under the Convention include all limitations on source-based taxation under Articles 6 through 22, the treaty-based relief from double taxation provided by Article 24 (Relief from Double Taxation), and the protection afforded to residents of a Contracting State under Article 25 (Non-discrimination). Some provisions do not require that a person be a resident in order to enjoy the benefits of those provisions. For example, Article 19 (Government Service) may apply to an employee of a Contracting State who is resident in neither State. Article 26 (Mutual Agreement Procedure) is not limited to residents of the Contracting States, and Article 28 (Diplomatic Agents and Consular Officers) applies to diplomatic agents or consular officials regardless of residence. Article 23 accordingly does not limit the availability of treaty benefits under these provisions.

Paragraph 2

Paragraph 2 has seven subparagraphs, each of which describes a category of residents that constitute "qualified persons" and thus are entitled to all benefits of the Convention. It is intended that the provisions of paragraph 2 will be self-executing. Claiming benefits under paragraph 2 does not require advance competent authority ruling or approval. The tax authorities may, of course, on review, determine that the taxpayer has improperly interpreted the paragraph and is not entitled to the benefits claimed.

<u>Individuals -- Subparagraph 2(a)</u>

Subparagraph (a) provides that individual residents of a Contracting State will be entitled to all treaty benefits. If such an individual receives income as a nominee on behalf of a third country resident, benefits may be denied under the respective articles of the Convention by the requirement that the beneficial owner of the income be a resident of a Contracting State.

<u>Qualified Governmental Entities -- Subparagraph 2(b)</u>

Subparagraph (b) provides that qualified governmental entities, as defined in subparagraph 1(k) of Article 3 (Definitions), also will be entitled to all benefits of the Convention. As described in Article 3, in addition to federal, state and local governments, the term "qualified governmental entity" encompasses certain government-owned corporations and other entities.

<u>Publicly-Traded Corporations -- Subparagraph 2(c)</u>

Subparagraph (c) of paragraph 2 applies to two categories of companies: publicly traded companies and subsidiaries of publicly traded companies. Clause (i) of subparagraph (c) generally provides that a company will be a qualified person if the principal class of its shares is listed on a recognized U.S. or U.K. stock exchange and is regularly traded on one or more recognized stock exchanges.

The term "recognized stock exchange" is defined in subparagraph (a) of paragraph 7 as (1) the NASDAQ System owned by the National Association of Securities Dealers and any stock exchange registered with the Securities and Exchange Commission as a national securities exchange for purposes of the Securities Exchange Act of 1934; (2) the London Stock Exchange and any other recognized investment exchange within the meaning of the Financial Services Act 1986 or the Financial Services and Markets Act 2000; (3) the Irish Stock Exchange, the Swiss Stock Exchange and the stock exchanges of Amsterdam, Brussels, Frankfurt, Hamburg, Johannesburg, Madrid, Milan, Paris, Stockholm, Sydney, Tokyo, Toronto, and Vienna; and (4) any other stock exchange agreed upon by the competent authorities of the Contracting States.

The term "principal class of shares" is defined in subparagraph (b) of paragraph 7. Clause (i) defines the term to mean the common shares of the company representing the majority of the aggregate voting power and value of the company. If the company does not have a class of ordinary or common shares representing the majority of the aggregate voting power and value of the company, then the "principal class of shares" is that class or any combination of classes of shares that represents, in the aggregate, a majority of the voting power and value of the company. In addition, clause (ii) of subparagraph (b) defines the term "shares" to include depository receipts for shares or trust certificates for shares.

A class of shares will be "regularly traded" in a taxable period, under subparagraph (e) of paragraph 7, if the aggregate number of shares of that class traded on one or more recognized exchanges during the twelve months ending on the day before the beginning of that taxable period is at least six percent of the average number of shares outstanding in that class during that twelve-month period. For this purpose, the notes provide that if a class of shares was not listed on a recognized stock exchange during this twelve-month period, the class of shares will be treated as regularly traded only if the class meets the aggregate trading requirements for the taxable period in which the income arises. Trading on one or more recognized stock exchanges may be aggregated for purposes of meeting the "regularly traded" standard of subparagraph (e). For example, a U.S. company could satisfy the definition of "regularly traded" through trading, in whole or in part, on a recognized stock exchange located in the United Kingdom or certain third countries. Authorized but unissued shares are not considered for purposes of subparagraph (e).

A company resident in a Contracting State is entitled to the benefits of the Convention under clause (ii) of subparagraph (c) of paragraph 2 if five or fewer direct and indirect owners of at least 50 percent of the aggregate vote and value of the company's shares are publicly traded companies described in clause (i). Thus, for example, a U.K. company, all the shares of which are owned by another U.K. company, would qualify for benefits under the Convention if the principal class of shares of the U.K. parent company were listed on the London Stock Exchange and regularly traded on the Irish stock exchange. However, the U.K. company would not qualify for benefits under clause (ii) if the publicly traded parent company were a resident of Ireland, not of the United States or the United Kingdom. Furthermore, if the U.K. parent indirectly owned the U.K. company through a chain of subsidiaries, each such subsidiary in the chain, as an intermediate owner, must be a resident of the United States or the United Kingdom for the U.K. company to meet the test in clause (ii).

This test differs from that under subparagraph 2(c)(i) in that 50 percent of each class of the company's shares, not merely the class or classes accounting for more than 50 percent of the company's votes and value, must be held by publicly-traded companies described in subparagraph 2(c)(i). Thus, the test under subparagraph 2(c)(ii) considers the ownership of every class of shares outstanding, while the test under subparagraph 2(c)(i) only considers those classes that account for a majority of the company's voting power and value. However, both subparagraphs are subject to the rules of paragraph 5, relating to certain arrangements pursuant to which holders of a class of stock in a resident of a Contracting State receive a disproportionate share of the income arising from the other Contracting State.

The rules of paragraph 5 may interact with the rules of this paragraph in order to deny benefits in whole or in part. The following example illustrates this interaction.

Example. UKCo is a corporation resident in the United Kingdom. UKCo has two classes of shares: Common and Preferred. The Common shares are listed on the London Stock Exchange and are substantially and regularly traded. The Preferred shares have no voting rights and are entitled to receive dividends equal in amount to interest payments that UKCo receives from unrelated borrowers in the United States. The Preferred shares are owned entirely by a single investor that is a resident of a country with which the United States does not have a tax treaty. The Common shares account for more than 50 percent of the value of UKCo and for 100 percent of the voting power. Because the owner of the Preferred shares is entitled to receive payments corresponding to the U.S. source interest income earned by UKCo, the Preferred shares are subject to the rules of paragraph 5. Because the owner of the Preferred shares is not an "equivalent beneficiary" within the meaning of subparagraph 7(d), UKCo will be denied benefits with respect to a portion of the interest payments. Benefits will be denied to the extent that the owner of the Preferred shares receives a greater proportion of the U.S. income than he would have received had he owned comparable Common shares.

Publicly-Traded Persons -- Subparagraph 2(d)

Subparagraph (d) of paragraph 2 applies to two categories of person that are not individuals or companies under the laws of one of the Contracting States: publicly traded entities and entities owned either by publicly traded companies or by publicly traded entities that are not companies. Clause (i) of subparagraph (d) provides that a person other than a company will be a qualified person if the principal class of "units" in that person is listed on a recognized U.S. or U.K. stock exchange and is regularly traded on one or more recognized stock exchanges.

With respect to a person, the term "units" is defined in subparagraph (c) of paragraph 7 as shares and any other instrument, other than debt claims, granting an entitlement to share in the assets or income of, or receive a distribution from, the person. The term "principal class of units" means the class of units which represents the majority of the value of the person. If no single class of units represents such a majority, the "principal class of units" is any combination of classes that, in the aggregate, represent more than fifty percent of the value of the person. The term "regularly traded," for purposes of subparagraph (d) of paragraph 2, is defined in subparagraph (e) of paragraph 7, as described above. Trading on one or more recognized stock exchanges may be aggregated for purposes of this requirement and authorized but unissued units are not considered for purposes of subparagraph (d).

A person other than an individual or a company is a qualified person under clause (ii) of subparagraph (d) if the direct or indirect owners of at least fifty percent of the beneficial interests in the entity are entities that satisfy the publicly traded test of subparagraphs (c) or (d). Thus, for example, a U.K. trust, a majority of the shares of ownership in which are owned by a second U.K. trust, would be a qualified person if the principal class of units of the second U.K. trust were listed on the London Stock Exchange and regularly traded on the Irish Stock Exchange. However, the first U.K. trust would not qualify for benefits under clause (ii) if the second U.K. trust were a resident of Ireland, not of the United States or the United Kingdom.

Subparagraph (d) applies generally to trusts the shares of ownership in which are publicly traded and to trusts that are owned by publicly traded entities. From the U.S. perspective, this provision relating to publicly traded trusts is redundant, since the United States would generally consider such trusts to be companies covered by the parallel provision under subparagraph (c).

The rules of paragraph 5 may interact with the rules of this paragraph in order to deny benefits in whole or in part. The following example illustrates this interaction.

Example 1. UKT1 is a U.K. unit investment trust that was organized to invest in U.S. stocks. It is one of a family of unit investment trusts organized by the same investment manager, each of which invests in stocks of a single country. Investors who want a diversified global portfolio invest in UKT2, a unit investment trust that holds a controlling interest in each of the individual country funds and is regularly traded on the London Stock Exchange. UKT2 owns 60 percent of UKT1's outstanding units; the rest are widely held. UKT1 qualifies for benefits.

Example 2. UKT1 is a U.K. unit investment trust that holds a diversified global portfolio of stocks. UKT2 is a unit investment trust that owns 60 percent of the units in UKT1. UKT2 issues a number of classes of units to accommodate the investment strategies of its unitholders. It lists all of its classes of units on the London Stock Exchange and meets the regular trading test. One class of units tracks the performance of a portfolio of U.S. technology companies. Since UKT2 controls UKT1, and the holders of that class of units will receive a disproportionate share of UKT1's income from U.S. sources, paragraph 5 will apply. Accordingly, UKT1 will be denied benefits with respect to a portion of the income received with respect to the technology companies in the portfolio if a majority of that class of shares is owned by persons who are not equivalent beneficiaries within the meaning of paragraph 7(d).

Tax Exempt Organizations -- Subparagraph 2(e)

Subparagraph (e) of paragraph 2 provides rules by which the tax-exempt organizations described in paragraph 3 of Article 4 (Residence) may be "qualified persons." A tax-exempt pension scheme or employee benefit arrangement described in subparagraphs (a) or (b) of paragraph 3 of Article 4 is a qualified person if more than fifty percent of the beneficiaries, members or participants of the organization are individuals resident in either Contracting State. For purposes of this provision, the term "beneficiaries" should be understood to refer to the persons receiving benefits from the organization. On the other hand, a tax-exempt organization described in subparagraph (c) of paragraph 3 of Article 4 (Residence) is automatically a qualified person, without regard to the residence of its beneficiaries or members. Entities qualifying under this subparagraph generally are those that are exempt from tax in their State of residence and that are organized and operated exclusively to fulfill religious, charitable, scientific, artistic, cultural, or educational purposes.

Ownership/Base Erosion -- Subparagraph 2(f)

Subparagraph 2(f) provides an additional test that applies to any form of legal entity that is a resident of a Contracting State. This test would not apply to U.K. trusts since the trust itself is not subject to tax as a resident of the United Kingdom; instead the United Kingdom taxes the trustee of the trust. U.S. complex trusts would be treated as residents of the United States because they are subject to tax in their own right. Such trusts therefore could claim benefits under this test or the test provided in subparagraph (g) that is specific to trusts.

The test provided in subparagraph (f), the so-called ownership and base erosion test, is a two-part test. Both prongs of the test must be satisfied for the resident to be entitled to benefits under subparagraph 2(f).

The ownership prong of the test, under clause (i), requires that 50 percent or more of the aggregate voting power and value of the person be owned directly or indirectly on at least half the days of the person's taxable year by persons who are themselves qualified persons under certain other tests of paragraph 2—subparagraphs (a), (b), or (e), or clause (i) of subparagraphs (c) or (d).

Trusts may be entitled to benefits under this provision if they are treated as residents under Article 4 (Residence) and they otherwise satisfy the requirements of this subparagraph. For purposes of this subparagraph, the beneficial interests in a trust will be considered to be owned by its beneficiaries in proportion to each beneficiary's actuarial interest in the trust. The interest of a remainder beneficiary will be equal to 100 percent less the aggregate percentages held by income beneficiaries. A beneficiary's interest in a trust will not be considered to be owned by a person entitled to benefits under the other provisions of paragraph 2 if it is not possible to determine the beneficiary's actuarial interest. Consequently, if it is not possible to determine the actuarial interest of any beneficiaries in a trust, the ownership test under clause i) cannot be satisfied, unless all possible beneficiaries are persons entitled to benefits under the other subparagraphs of paragraph 2.

The base erosion prong of clause (ii) of subparagraph (f) disqualifies a person if fifty percent or more of the person's gross income for the taxable period is paid or accrued to a person or persons who are not residents of either Contracting State, in the form of payments deductible for tax purposes in the payer's State of residence. For this purpose, the notes state that the term "gross income" means total revenues derived by a resident of a Contracting State from its principal operations, less the direct costs of obtaining such revenues. In the case of the United States, the term "gross income" has the same meaning as such term in section 61 of the Code and the regulations thereunder.

To the extent they are deductible from the taxable base, trust distributions are deductible payments. However, depreciation and amortization deductions, which do not represent payments or accruals to other persons, are disregarded for this purpose. Deductible payments also do not include arm's length payments in the ordinary course of business for services or tangible property or with respect to financial obligations to banks that are residents of either Contracting State, or that have a permanent establishment in either Contracting State to which the payment is attributable.

The rules of paragraph 5 may interact with the rules of this paragraph as they apply to companies in order to deny benefits in whole or in part. The following example illustrates this interaction.

Example. A group of U.K. resident individuals established an investment club. The investment club purchases stocks through HoldCo, a U.K. company owned by the U.K. resident individuals in proportion to their contributions to the investment club. The rules of the investment club prevent the club from borrowing. One of the club's investments was an 80 percent interest in a U.S. biotech company, USCo, which was made in early 1997. USCo developed an unusual gene therapy, resulting in a substantial increase in the value of USCo stock. The members of the club wanted to sell some of the shares of USCo in order to diversify their holdings, but did not want to be subject to capital gains tax in the United Kingdom. Instead, HoldCo issued a class of preferred shares that track the dividends paid by USCo to HoldCo in exchange for a capital contribution from Investor. Investor is an individual resident in another EU member country. HoldCo meets the test for eligibility for the zero rate of withholding tax under paragraph 3(a) of Article 10 because it qualifies for benefits under the ownership-base erosion test and it has owned a direct 80 percent interest in USCo since before October 1, 1998. However, HoldCo would not be entitled to a zero rate of withholding tax on a portion of the dividends paid by USCo to the extent the preferred shares result in Investor receiving its proportionate share of the income of HoldCo since Investor is not an equivalent beneficiary within the meaning of paragraph 7(d).

Trusts -- Subparagraph (g)

Subparagraph (g) of paragraph 2 provides an additional means by which a trust can be a "qualified person." A trust or its trustee (acting in its capacity as such) will be a "qualified person" if the trust meets an ownership test and a base erosion test. The United Kingdom asked that this test be included because it was unclear how each country would apply the standard "ownership-base erosion" test of subparagraph (f) to trusts, since the United Kingdom treats the trustee as the taxpayer with respect to trusts. U.S. complex trusts, which are taxpayers in their own right, could also qualify under the ownership-base erosion test of subparagraph (f) if there were some advantage to applying that test rather than the test of subparagraph (g).

Under the ownership test, at least 50 percent of the beneficial interest in the trust must be held by certain qualified persons or, alternatively, by "equivalent beneficiaries." The qualified persons that satisfy the ownership test of subparagraph (g) generally are individuals, qualified governmental entities, publicly-traded companies or entities, and tax-exempt organizations.

The term "equivalent beneficiary" is defined in subparagraph (d) of paragraph 7. This definition may be met in two alternative ways, the first of which has two requirements.

Under the first alternative, a person may be an equivalent beneficiary because it is entitled to equivalent benefits under a treaty between the country of source and the country in which the person is a resident. This alternative has two requirements.

The first requirement is that the person must be a resident of a Member State of the European Community, a European Economic Area state, or a party to the North American Free Trade Agreement (collectively, "qualifying States").

The second requirement is that the person must be entitled to equivalent benefits under an applicable treaty. To satisfy this requirement, the person must be entitled to all the benefits of a comprehensive treaty between the Contracting State from which benefits of the Convention are claimed and a qualifying State. For this purpose, however, if the treaty in question does not have a comprehensive limitation on benefits article, this requirement only is met if the person would be a "qualified person" under the tests in Paragraph 2 applicable to individuals, qualified governmental entities, publicly-traded companies or entities, and tax-exempt organizations. In addition, with respect to dividends, interest, or royalties, the person must be entitled to a rate of tax that is at least as low as the rate that would apply under the Convention to such income.

The second alternative for satisfying the "equivalent beneficiary" test is available only to residents of one of the two Contracting States. U.S. or U.K. residents who are qualified persons by reason of subparagraphs a), b), c)(i), d)(i), or e) of paragraph 2 are equivalent beneficiaries for purposes of the relevant tests in Article 23. Thus, a U.K. individual will be an equivalent beneficiary without regard to whether the individual would have been entitled to receive the same benefits if it received the income directly. A resident of a third country cannot be a "qualified person" by reason of those paragraphs or any other rule of the treaty, and therefore do not qualify as equivalent beneficiaries under this alternative. Thus, any resident of a third country can be an equivalent beneficiary only if it would have been entitled to equivalent benefits had it received the income directly.

For example, assume that a U.S. company pays interest to UKT, a trust resident in the United Kingdom. UKT has three equal beneficiaries, a U.K. resident individual and two individuals resident in Italy. The U.K. individual is an equivalent beneficiary by reason of Article 23(7)(d)(ii). However, the Italian individuals are not equivalent beneficiaries since, if each had received directly his share of the interest, that portion would be subject to a withholding tax of fifteen percent under the income tax treaty between the United States and Italy. This rate is higher than the rate that would apply under the Convention. Therefore, UKT does not meet the second requirement by virtue of clause (i) of subparagraph (d).

The base erosion test of subparagraph (g) of paragraph 2 is similar to the base erosion test in clause (ii) of subparagraph (f) of paragraph 2. A trust or trustee meets the base erosion test in subparagraph (g) if less than 50 percent of its gross income for the taxable period is paid or accrued, directly or indirectly, to a person or persons who are not residents of either Contracting State in the form of payments deductible for tax purposes in the trust or trustee's State of residence. As in the case of the subparagraph (f) base erosion test, deductible payments do not include arm's length payments in the ordinary course of business for services or tangible property or with respect to financial obligations to banks that are residents of either Contracting State or that have a permanent establishment in either Contracting State to which the payment is attributable. For this purpose, the notes state that the term "gross income" means total revenues derived by a resident of a Contracting State from its principal operations, less the direct costs of obtaining such revenues. In the case of the United States, the term "gross income" has the same meaning as such term in section 61 of the Code and the regulations thereunder.

☐☐☐☐*g*☐☐☐☐☐☐☐

Paragraph 3 sets forth a derivative benefits test that applies to all treaty benefits. In general, a derivative benefits test entitles the resident of a Contracting State to treaty benefits if the owner of the resident would have been entitled to the same benefit had the income in question flowed directly to that owner. Paragraph 3 provides a derivative benefits test under which a company that is a resident of a Contracting State may be entitled to the benefits of the Convention with respect to certain items of income. To qualify under this paragraph, the company must meet an ownership test and a base erosion test.

Subparagraph (a) sets forth the ownership test. Under this test, seven or fewer equivalent beneficiaries must own shares representing at least 95 percent of the aggregate voting power and value of the company. Ownership may be direct or indirect. The term "equivalent beneficiary" is defined in subparagraph (d) of paragraph 7. This definition may be met in two alternative ways, the first of which has two requirements.

Under the first alternative, a person may be an equivalent beneficiary because it is entitled to equivalent benefits under a treaty between the country of source and the country in which the person is a resident. This alternative has two requirements.

The first requirement is that the person must be a resident of a Member State of the European Community, a European Economic Area state, or a party to the North American Free Trade Agreement (collectively, "qualifying States").

The second requirement of the definition of "equivalent beneficiary" is that the person must be entitled to equivalent benefits under an applicable treaty. To satisfy the second requirement, the person must be entitled to all the benefits of a comprehensive treaty between the Contracting State from which benefits of the Convention are claimed and a qualifying State. For this purpose, however, if the treaty in question does not have a comprehensive limitation on benefits article, this requirement only is met if the person would be a "qualified person" under the tests in Paragraph 2 applicable to individuals, qualified governmental entities, publicly-traded companies or entities, and tax-exempt organizations. In addition, to satisfy the second requirement by virtue of clause (i) of subparagraph (d) with respect to dividends, interest, or royalties, the person must be entitled to a rate of tax that is at least as low as the rate that would apply under the Convention to such income.

In order to satisfy the additional requirement necessary to qualify as an "equivalent beneficiary" under paragraph 7(d)(i) with respect to dividends, interest, or royalties, the person must be entitled to a rate of withholding tax that is at least as low as the withholding tax rate that would apply under the Convention to such income. Thus, the rates to be compared are: (1) the rate of withholding tax that the source State would have imposed if a qualified resident of the other Contracting State was the beneficially owner of the income; and (2) the rate of withholding tax that the source State would have imposed if the third State resident received the income directly from the source State. For example, USCo is a wholly owned subsidiary of UKCo, a company resident in the United Kingdom. UKCo is wholly owned by FCo, a corporation resident in France. Assuming UKCo satisfies the requirements of paragraph 3(a) of Article 10 (Dividends), UKCo would be eligible for a zero rate of withholding tax. The dividend withholding rate in the treaty between the United States and France is 5 percent. Thus, if FCo received the dividend directly from USCo, FCo would have been subject to a 5 percent rate of withholding tax on the dividend. Because FCo would not be entitled to a rate of withholding tax that is at least as low as the rate that would apply under the Convention to such income (Le., zero), FCo is not an equivalent beneficiary within the meaning of paragraph 7(d)(i) of Article 23 with respect to zero rate of withholding tax on dividends.

The requirement that a person be entitled to "all the benefits" of a comprehensive tax treaty eliminates those persons that qualify for benefits with respect to only certain types of income. Accordingly, the fact that a French parent of a U.K. company is engaged in the active conduct of a trade or business in France and therefore would be entitled to the benefits of the

86

U.S.-France treaty if it received dividends directly is not sufficient for purposes of this paragraph. Further, the French company cannot be an equivalent beneficiary if it qualifies for benefits only with respect to certain income as a result of a "derivative benefits" provision in the U.S.-France treaty. However, it would be possible to look through the French company to its parent company to determine whether the parent company is an equivalent beneficiary.

The following example illustrates the "all the benefits" requirement. A U.K. resident company, Y, owns all of the shares in a U.S. resident company, Z. Y is wholly owned by X, a German resident company that would not qualify for all of the benefits of the U.S.-Germany income tax treaty but may qualify for benefits with respect to certain items of income under the "active trade or business" test of the U.S.-Germany treaty. X, in turn, is wholly owned by W, a French resident company that is substantially and regularly traded on the Paris Stock Exchange. Z pays a dividend to Y. Y qualifies for benefits under paragraph 3 of Article 23, assuming that the requirements of subparagraph 3(b) of Article 23 are met. Y is directly owned by X, which is not an equivalent beneficiary within the meaning of subparagraph 7(d)(i) of Article 23 (X does not qualify for all of the benefits of the U.S.-Germany tax treaty). However, Y is also indirectly owned by W and W may be an equivalent beneficiary. Y would not be entitled to the zero rate of withholding tax on dividends available under the Convention because W is not an equivalent beneficiary with respect to the zero rate of withholding tax since W is not eligible for such rate under the U.S.-France income tax treaty. W qualifies as an equivalent beneficiary with respect to the 5 percent maximum rate of withholding tax because (a) it is a French resident company whose shares are substantially and regularly traded on a recognized stock exchange, within the meaning of the Limitation on Benefits Article of the U.S.-France income tax treaty and (b) the dividend withholding rate in the treaty between the United States and France is 5 percent. Accordingly, U.S. withholding tax on the dividend from Z to Y will be imposed at a rate of 5 percent in accordance with subparagraph 2(a) of Article 10.

The second alternative for satisfying the "equivalent beneficiary" test is available only to residents of one of the two Contracting States. U.S. or U.K. residents who are qualified persons by reason of subparagraphs a), b), c)(i), d)(i), or e) of paragraph 2 are equivalent beneficiaries for purposes of the relevant tests in Article 23. Thus, a U.K. individual will be an equivalent beneficiary without regard to whether the individual would have been entitled to receive the same benefits if it received the income directly. A resident of a third country cannot be a "qualified person" by reason of those paragraphs or any other rule of the treaty, and therefore do not qualify as equivalent beneficiaries under this alternative. Thus, any resident of a third country can be an equivalent beneficiary only if it would have been entitled to equivalent benefits had it received the income directly.

The second alternative was included in order to clarify that ownership by certain residents of a Contracting State would not disqualify a U.S. or U.K. company under this paragraph. Thus, for example, if 90 percent of a U.K. company is owned by five companies that are resident in member states of the European Union who satisfy the requirements of clause (i), and 10 percent of the U.K. company is owned by a U.S. or U.K. individual, then the U.K. company still can satisfy the requirements of subparagraph (a) of paragraph 3.

Subparagraph (b) sets forth the base erosion test. A company meets this base erosion test if less than 50 percent of its gross income for the taxable period is paid or accrued, directly or indirectly, to a person or persons who are not equivalent beneficiaries in the form of payments deductible for tax purposes in company's State of residence. This test is the same as the base erosion test in clause (ii) of subparagraph (f) of paragraph 2, except that deductible payments made to equivalent beneficiaries, rather than amounts paid to residents of a Contracting State, are not counted against a company for purposes of determining whether the company exceeded the 50 percent limit.

As in the case of base erosion test in subparagraph (f) of paragraph 2, deductible payments in subparagraph (b) of paragraph 3 also do not include arm's length payments in the ordinary course of business for services or tangible property or with respect to financial obligations to banks that are residents of either Contracting State or that have a permanent establishment in either Contracting State to which the payment is attributable. In addition, the notes define the term "gross income" for purposes of Article 23 as the total revenues derived by a resident of a Contracting State from its principal operations, less the direct costs of obtaining such revenues. This definition is consistent with that of section 61 of the Code and the regulations thereunder.

The rules of paragraph 5 may interact with the rules of this paragraph as they apply to companies in order to deny benefits in whole or in part. The following example illustrates this interaction.

Example. UKCo is a U.K. holding company, all the issued and outstanding stock of which is owned 50 percent by a privately-held Danish company, DCo, and 50 percent by a privately-held French company, FCo. UKCo, in turn, owns 75 percent of the issued and outstanding stock of USCo, a U.S. company engaged in the manufacture of wallpaper and jet fuel. UKCo pays less than 50 percent of its gross income to other persons in the form of payments deductible under U.K. law. DCo and FCo are approached by a Thai company, TCo, engaged in the business of wallpaper manufacture in Southeast Asia. DCo, FCo, and TCo arrange for UKCo to issue a class of preferred stock to TCo, in exchange for a capital contribution. Payments with respect to this class of preferred stock will be set at a fixed rate increased by the excess of the internal rate of return on USCo's wallpaper business over the yield on 30-year U.S. Treasury Bonds. UKCo would be entitled, under paragraph 3, to a 5 percent withholding rate with respect to distributions from USCo because DCo and FCo would have been entitled to the same withholding rate on a direct payment from USCo. However, UKCo will not be entitled to a 5 percent withholding rate on a portion of the dividends paid by USCo because of the preferred shares issued to TCo. TCo is not an equivalent beneficiary within the meaning of subparagraph (d) of paragraph 7 of Article 23.

□□□*g*□□□□□□□

Paragraph 4 sets forth a test under which a resident of a Contracting State that is not a "qualified person" under paragraph 2 may receive treaty benefits with respect to certain items of income that are connected to an active trade or business conducted in its State of residence.

Subparagraph (a) sets forth the general rule that a resident of a Contracting State engaged in the active conduct of a trade or business in that State may obtain the benefits of the Convention with respect to an item of income, profit, or gain derived in the other Contracting State. The item of income, profit, or gain, however, must be derived in connection with or incidental to that trade or business.

The term "trade or business" is not defined in the Convention. Pursuant to paragraph 2 of Article 3 (General Definitions), when determining whether a resident of the United Kingdom is entitled to the benefits of the Convention under paragraph 4 of this Article with respect to an item of income, profit, or gains derived from sources within the United States, the United States will ascribe to this term the meaning that it has under the law of the United States. Accordingly, the U.S. competent authority will refer to the regulations issued under section 367(a) for the definition of the term "trade or business." In general, therefore, a trade or business will be considered to be a specific unified group of activities that constitute or could constitute an independent economic enterprise carried on for profit. Furthermore, a corporation generally will be considered to carry on a trade or business only if the officers and employees of the corporation conduct substantial managerial and operational activities.

The business of making or managing investments for the resident's own account will be considered to be a trade or business only when part of banking, insurance or securities activities conducted by a bank, an insurance company, or a registered securities dealer. Such activities conducted by a person other than a bank, insurance company or registered securities dealer will not be considered to be the conduct of an active trade or business, nor would they be considered to be the conduct of an active trade or business if conducted by a bank, insurance company or registered securities dealer but not as part of the company's banking, insurance or dealer business.

For this purpose, subparagraph (f) of paragraph 7 defines the term "insurance company" as an incorporated or unincorporated entity if its gross income consists primarily of insurance or reinsurance premiums and investment income attributable to such premiums. For this purpose, the notes define the term "gross income" as the total revenues derived by a resident of a Contracting State from its principal operations, less the direct costs of obtaining such revenues. In the case of the United States, the term "gross income" has the same meaning as such term in section 61 of the Code and the regulations thereunder.

Because a headquarters operation is in the business of managing investments, a company that functions solely as a headquarters company will not be considered to be engaged in an active trade or business for purposes of subparagraph (a).

According to the notes, income, profit, or gain is derived in connection with a trade or business if the income-producing activity in the State of source is a line of business that "forms a part of" or is "complementary" to the trade or business conducted in the State of residence by the income recipient.

A business activity generally will be considered to form part of a business activity conducted in the State of source if the two activities involve the design, manufacture or sale of the same products or type of products, or the provision of similar services. The notes clarify that the line of business in the State of residence may be upstream, downstream, or parallel to the activity conducted in the State of source. Thus, the line of business may provide inputs for a manufacturing process that occurs in the State of source, may sell the output of that manufacturing process, or simply may sell the same sorts of products that are being sold by the trade or business carried on in the State of source.

Example 1. USCo is a corporation resident in the United States. USCo is engaged in an active manufacturing business in the United States. USCo owns 100 percent of the shares of UKCo, a company resident in the United Kingdom. UKCo distributes USCo products in the United Kingdom. Because the business activities conducted by the two corporations involve the same products, UKCo's distribution business is considered to form a part of USCo's manufacturing business.

Example 2. The facts are the same as in Example 1, except that USCo does not manufacture. Rather, USCo operates a large research and development facility in the United States that licenses intellectual property to affiliates worldwide, including UKCo. UKCo and other USCo affiliates then manufacture and market the USCo-designed products in their respective markets. Because the activities conducted by UKCo and USCo involve the same product lines, these activities are considered to form a part of the same trade or business.

For two activities to be considered to be "complementary," the activities need not relate to the same types of products or services, but they should be part of the same overall industry and be related in the sense that the success or failure of one activity will tend to result in success or failure for the other. Where more than one trade or business is conducted in the State of source and only one of the trades or businesses forms a part of or is complementary to a trade or business conducted in the State of residence, it is necessary to identify the trade or business to which an item of income is attributable. Royalties generally will be considered to be derived in connection with the trade or business to which the underlying intangible property is attributable. Dividends will be deemed to be derived first out of earnings and profits of the treaty-benefited trade or business, and then out of other earnings and profits. Interest income may be allocated under any reasonable method consistently applied. A method that conforms to U.S. principles for expense allocation will be considered a reasonable method.

Example 3. Americair is a corporation resident in the United States that operates an international airline. UKSub is a wholly-owned subsidiary of Americair resident in the United Kingdom. UKSub operates a chain of hotels in the United Kingdom that are located near airports served by Americair flights. Americair frequently sells tour packages that include air travel to the United Kingdom and lodging at UKSub hotels. Although both companies are engaged in the active conduct of a trade or business, the businesses of operating a chain of hotels and operating an airline are distinct trades or businesses. Therefore UKSub's business does not form a part of Americair's business. However, UKSub's business is considered to be complementary to Americair's business because they are part of the same overall industry (travel), and the links between their operations tend to make them interdependent.

Example 4. The facts are the same as in Example 3, except that UKSub owns an office building in the United Kingdom instead of a hotel chain. No part of Americair's business is conducted through the office building. UKSub's business is not considered to form a part of or to be complementary to Americair's business. They are engaged in distinct trades or businesses in separate industries, and there is no economic dependence between the two operations.

Example 5. USFlower is a company resident in the United States. USFlower produces and sells flowers in the United States and other countries. USFlower owns all the shares of UKHolding, a corporation resident in the United Kingdom. UKHolding is a holding company that is not engaged in a trade or business. UKHolding owns all the shares of three corporations that are resident in the United Kingdom: UKFlower, UKLawn, and UKFish. UKFlower distributes USFlower flowers under the USFlower trademark in the United Kingdom. UKLawn markets a line of lawn care products in the United Kingdom under the USFlower trademark. In addition to being sold under the same trademark, UKLawn and UKFlower products are sold in the same stores and sales of each company's products tend to generate increased sales of the other's products. UKFish imports fish from the United States and distributes it to fish wholesalers in the United Kingdom. For purposes of paragraph 4, the business of UKFlower forms a part of the business of USFlower, the business of UKLawn is complementary to the business of USFlower, and the business of UKFish is neither part of nor complementary to that of USFlower.

Finally, the notes provide that an item of income, profit, or gain derived from the State of source is "incidental to" the trade or business carried on in the State of residence if production of the item facilitates the conduct of the trade or business in the State of residence. An example of incidental income is the temporary investment of working capital of a person in the State of residence in securities issued by persons in the State of source.

Subparagraph (b) of paragraph 4 states a further condition to the general rule in subparagraph (a) in cases where the trade or business generating the item of income in question is carried on either by the person deriving the income or by any associated enterprises. Subparagraph (b) states that the trade or business carried on in the State of residence, under these circumstances, must be substantial in relation to the activity in the State of source. This determination is made based upon all the facts and circumstances and takes into account the comparative sizes of the trades or businesses in each Contracting State (measured by reference to asset values, income and payroll expenses), the nature of the activities performed in each Contracting State, and the relative contributions made to that trade or business in each Contracting State. In making each determination or comparison, due regard will be given to the relative sizes of the U.S. and U.K. economies.

The determination in subparagraph (b) also is made separately for each item of income derived from the State of source. It therefore is possible that a person would be entitled to the benefits of the Convention with respect to one item of income but not with respect to another. If a resident of a Contracting State is entitled to treaty benefits with respect to a particular item of income under paragraph 4, the resident is entitled to all benefits of the Convention insofar as they affect the taxation of that item of income in the State of source.

The substantiality requirement is intended to prevent a narrow case of treaty-shopping abuses in which a company attempts to qualify for benefits by engaging in de minimis connected business activities in the treaty country in which it is resident (□e., activities that have little economic cost or effect with respect to the company business as a whole).

The application of the substantiality test only to income from related parties focuses only on potential abuse cases, and does not hamper certain other kinds of non-abusive activities, even though the income recipient resident in a Contracting State may be very small in relation to the entity generating income in the other Contracting State. For example, if a small U.S. research firm develops a process that it license to a very large, unrelated, U.K. pharmaceutical manufacturer, the size of the U.S. research firm would not have to be tested against the size of the U.K. manufacturer. Similarly, a small U.S. bank that makes a loan to a very large unrelated U.K. business would not have to pass a substantiality test to receive treaty benefits under subparagraph (b).

Subparagraph (c) of paragraph 4 provides special rules for determining whether a resident of a Contracting State is engaged in the active conduct of a trade or business within the meaning of subparagraph (a). Subparagraph (c) attributes the activities of a partnership to each of its partners. Subparagraph (c) also attributes to a person activities conducted by persons "connected" to such person. A person ("X") is connected to another person ("Y") if X possesses 50 percent or more of the beneficial interest in Y (or if Y possesses 50 percent or more of the beneficial interest in X). For this purpose, X is connected to a company if X owns shares representing fifty percent or more of the aggregate voting power and value of the company or fifty percent or more of the beneficial equity interest in the company. X also is connected to Y if a third person possesses fifty percent or more of the beneficial interest in both X and Y. For this purpose, if X or Y is a company, the threshold relationship with respect to such company or companies is fifty percent or more of the aggregate voting power and value or fifty percent or more of the beneficial equity interest. Finally, X is connected to Y if, based upon all the facts and circumstances, X controls Y, Y controls X, or X and Y are controlled by the same person or persons.

□□□*g*□□□□□

Paragraph 5 denies the benefits of the Convention to the disproportionate part of the income earned by certain companies. A company is subject to paragraph 5 if it meets two tests, set forth in subparagraphs (a) and (b) of paragraph 5. A company resident in a Contracting State meets the test of subparagraph (a) if it has outstanding a class of shares which is subject to terms or other arrangements which entitle the holder to a larger portion of the company's income, profit, or gain in the other Contracting State than the holder otherwise would be entitled in the absence of such terms or arrangements. Thus, for example, a company resident in the United Kingdom meets the test of subparagraph (a) if it has outstanding a class of "tracking stock" that pays dividends based upon a formula that approximates the company's return on its assets employed in the United States.

The disproportionate part of the income of the company is the excess portion of the company's income, profit, or gain from the other Contracting State to which the holders are entitled, above what they otherwise would be entitled. So-called alphabet stock that entitles the holder to earnings in the State produced by a particular division of the company would cause a company to be subject to the rule of paragraph 5.

Example 1. UKCo is a company resident in the United Kingdom that specializes in food products. UKCo has two classes of shares: Common and Class S Common. The Common shares are listed on the London Stock Exchange and are substantially and regularly traded. Class S Common is so-called tracking stock. Accordingly, the dividends on Class S Common are equal to the earnings and profits of Software Co., a U.S. subsidiary of UKCo. Dividends cannot be paid on Class S shares if UKCo does not have sufficient earnings and profits; otherwise, the return on Class S shares is independent of the performance of UKCo's food business. The Class S shares were created by UKCo because it felt that the stock market did not appropriately value the contribution that Software Co. made to the UKCo group. Because the holders of the Class S Common shares are entitled to receive payments corresponding to the earnings and profits of Software Co., a U.S. company, UKCo is subject to paragraph 5 with respect to dividends received from Software Co.

Example 2. UKCo is a corporation resident in the United Kingdom. UKCo has two classes of shares: Common and Preferred. The Common shares are listed on the London Stock Exchange and are substantially and regularly traded. The Preferred shares have no voting rights and are entitled to receive dividends equal in amount to the income earned by UKCo from selling widgets in the United Kingdom. Because the Preferred shares do not entitle the owner to receive dividends or other payments corresponding to U.S.-source income received by UKCo, the Preferred shares are not considered a disproportionate class of shares.

A company meets the test of subparagraph (b) if fifty percent or more of the voting power and value of the class of shares is owned by persons who are not "equivalent beneficiaries." The term "equivalent beneficiary" is defined in subparagraph (d) of paragraph 7, discussed above in connection with subparagraph (g) of paragraph 2 and subparagraph (a) of paragraph 3.

□□□□g□□□□□□

Paragraph 6 provides that a resident of one of the States that is neither a qualified person nor entitled to the benefits of the Convention with respect to an item of income, profit, or gain under paragraphs 3 or 4 of this article still may be granted benefits under the Convention at the discretion of the competent authority of the State from which benefits are claimed. In making determinations under paragraph 6, that competent authority will take into account as its guideline whether the establishment, acquisition, or maintenance of the person seeking benefits under the Convention, or the conduct of such person's operations, has or had as one of its principal purposes the obtaining of benefits under the Convention. Thus, persons that establish operations in one of the States with a principal purpose of obtaining the benefits of the Convention ordinarily will not be granted relief under paragraph 6.

The competent authority may determine to grant all benefits of the Convention, or it may determine to grant only certain benefits. For instance, it may determine to grant benefits only with respect to a particular item of income in a manner similar to paragraph (3). Further, the competent authority may set time limits on the duration of any relief granted.

For purposes of implementing paragraph 6, a taxpayer will be permitted to present his case to the relevant competent authority for an advance determination based on the facts. In these circumstances, it is also expected that if the competent authority determines that benefits are to be allowed, they will be allowed retroactively to the time of entry into force of the relevant treaty provision or the establishment of the structure in question, whichever is later. A competent authority is required by paragraph 6 to consult the other competent authority before denying benefits under this paragraph.

According to the notes, the competent authorities will consider the respective obligations of the United Kingdom and the United States by virtue of their membership in the European Community and the European Economic Area on the one hand, and the North American Free Trade Agreement on the other, in making a determination under paragraph 6. In particular, the competent authorities will consider any legal requirements for the facilitation of the free movement of capital and persons, the differing internal tax systems, tax incentive regimes and existing tax treaty policies among Member States of the European Community or European Economic Area states, or parties to the North American Free Trade Agreement (collectively, the "qualifying States"). As a result, where certain changes in circumstances otherwise might cause a person to cease to be a qualified person under paragraph 2 of this article, such changes need not result in the denial of benefits.

The competent authorities thus will take into account the legal requirements for the free flow of goods and services within the European Communities and within the North American Free Trade Area. The changes in circumstances contemplated by the notes include, all under ordinary business conditions, a change in the State of residence of a major participant in a company; the sale of part of the ownership interests in a company to a resident of a qualifying State; or an expansion of a company's activities in another qualifying State. So long as the relevant competent authority is satisfied that those changed circumstances are not attributable to tax avoidance motives, they will count as a factor favoring the granting of benefits under paragraph 6, if consistent with existing treaty policies, such as the need for effective exchange of information. See the Technical Explanation to paragraph 3 of Article 10 for a discussion of the factors that the competent authority will consider in making these determinations. A company that wishes the relevant competent authority to take such legal requirements into account must request an advance determination, as described above.

☐☐☐*g*☐☐☐☐☐☐

Paragraph 7 defines several key terms for purposes of Article 23. Each of the defined terms is discussed in the context in which it is used. Subparagraphs (a), (b), (c), and (e) of paragraph 7 are discussed in connection with paragraph 2. Subparagraph (d) is discussed in connection with paragraphs 2, 3 and 5. Subparagraph (f) is discussed in connection with paragraph 4.

Article 24 (Relief from Double Taxation)

This Article describes the manner in which each Contracting State undertakes to relieve double taxation. The United States uses the foreign tax credit method under its internal law and by treaty.

The notes contain special rules for the application of Article 24 to fiscally transparent entities in order to allocate primary and residual taxing rights between the two Contracting States. Clarifications are necessary because the Contracting States may have different views regarding the identity of the taxpayer. Under paragraph 4 or 8 of Article 1, a Contracting State may tax an entity as a resident even though the other Contracting State views the entity as fiscally transparent (*e.g.*, as a partnership) and taxes its own residents on the same income. In such cases, the tax generally will be treated as being paid by the citizen or resident of the first-mentioned Contracting State for purposes of Article 24. The effect is to give primary taxing rights to the State in which the entity is a resident, and ensure that double tax is relieved by having the other State give a foreign tax credit for the taxes paid by the entity.

For example, a U.K. company pays interest to a U.K. unlimited liability company ("ULC") with U.S. resident partners. The ULC has elected to be treated for U.S. tax purposes as a partnership. Under Article 11 (Interest), the U.S. partners claim an exemption from U.K. withholding tax with respect to that interest. However, because the United Kingdom treats the ULC as a company resident in the United Kingdom for U.K. tax purposes, the saving clause of paragraph 4 of Article 1 ensures that the United Kingdom may continue to tax the company as a U.K. resident. Pursuant to the notes, the United States will treat the tax paid by the ULC as having been paid by the partners for purposes of providing a foreign tax credit to the U.S. partners with respect to the interest income.

An exception to this rule for fiscally transparent entities is provided in cases involving real property, since primary taxing rights with respect to income from real property always rest with the State in which the property is located. To ensure that primary taxing rights remain with the situs state, in cases involving income from real property subject to paragraph 1 of Article 6 (Income from Real Property) or gain from the alienation of real property subject to paragraph 1 of Article 13 (Gains), tax paid by a resident of the Contracting State in which the real property is located will be treated as paid by a resident of the other Contracting State.

For example, a U.K. unlimited liability company ("ULC") with U.S. resident partners derives gain from the sale of U.S. real property. The ULC has elected to be treated for U.S. tax purposes as a partnership and, therefore, the U.S. taxes the U.S. resident partners on the gain derived. However, because the United Kingdom treats the ULC as a company resident in the United Kingdom, the saving clause of paragraph 4 of Article 1 (General Scope) ensures that the United Kingdom may continue to tax the company as a U.K. resident. Because the notes provide that the United States retains primary taxing rights with respect to real property located in the United States, the United Kingdom will treat the tax paid by the U.S. resident partners as having been paid by the ULC for purposes of providing the foreign tax credit to the ULC with respect to the gain derived from the sale of U.S. real property.

The same rule applies with respect to a trust taxable as an entity. A U.S. company pays interest to a U.S. complex trust ("UST") with U.K. beneficiaries. The UST is treated for U.K. tax purposes as fiscally transparent entity. Under Article 11 (Interest), the U.K. beneficiaries claim an exemption from U.S. withholding tax with respect to that interest. However, because the United States treats the UST as a taxable entity resident in the United States for U.S. tax purposes, the saving clause of paragraph 4 of Article 1 ensures that the United States may continue to tax the trust as a U.S. resident. Pursuant to the notes, the United Kingdom will treat the tax paid by the UST as having been paid by the U.K. beneficiaries for purposes of providing a foreign tax credit to the U.K. beneficiaries with respect to the interest income.

The notes contain additional rules for the application of Article 24 where an item of income, profit, or gain is derived through a grantor or settlor trust, and each Contracting State considers the income, profit or gain to be derived by different persons resident in each State. For example, if a trust is a grantor trust for U.S. tax purposes, the income of the trust is included in the income of the U.S. grantor, and the grantor is taxed on the income. However, for U.K. tax purposes the trust income may be included in the income of the beneficiaries of the trust so that the beneficiaries pay tax on the income in the U.K. Thus, each country will have a different view regarding the identity of the taxpayer and, without a special rule, double taxation may occur with respect to that income.

The notes provide that if the person taxed by one State is the grantor of the trust, and the person taxed in the other State is a beneficiary of the trust, the tax paid or accrued by the beneficiary will be treated as if it were paid or accrued by the grantor for the purposes of determining the relief from double taxation allowed by the State of which the grantor is a resident. Thus, in the case of the trust described above, the United States would provide a credit to the U.S. grantor for the U.K. tax imposed upon the U.K. beneficiaries of the trust. An exception to this special rule applies with respect to an in item of income from real property to which paragraph 1 of Article 6 applies, or gain from the alienation of real property to which paragraph 1 of Article 13 applies. If the item in question is income from real property or gain from the alienation of real property, the tax paid by the resident of the Contracting State in which the property is located will be treated as if it were paid by the person who is a resident of the other Contracting State. Thus, the Contracting State in which the real property is located will have the primary taxing jurisdiction over the property and the other Contracting State will allow relief from double taxation.

The re-sourcing rules of paragraphs 2 and 5, described below, will apply to the extent necessary to provide relief from double taxation.

□□□g□□□□□

The United States agrees, in subparagraph (a) of paragraph 1, to allow to its citizens and residents a credit against U.S. tax for income taxes paid or accrued to the United Kingdom. For this purpose, the taxes covered by subparagraph (b) of paragraph 3 and by paragraph 4 of Article 2 (Taxes Covered) are income taxes. Thus, the U.K. income tax, capital gains tax, corporation tax, and petroleum revenue tax (subject to paragraph 3 of this article), as well as any identical or substantially similar U.K. taxes that are imposed after the date of signature of the

Convention in addition to, or in place of, these existing taxes, are considered to be income taxes for purposes of paragraph 1. The granting of a foreign tax credit with respect to U.K. taxes is based on the Treasury Department's review of the laws of the United Kingdom.

Subparagraph (b) provides for a deemed-paid credit, consistent with section 902 of the Code to a U.S. corporation in respect of dividends received from a corporation resident in the United Kingdom of which the U.S. corporation owns at least 10 percent of the voting stock. This credit is for the tax paid by the corporation of the United Kingdom on the profits out of which the dividends are considered paid.

The credits allowed under paragraph 1 are allowed in accordance with the provisions and subject to the limitations of U.S. law, as that law may be amended over time, so long as the general principle of the Article, that is, the allowance of a credit, is retained. Thus, although the Convention provides for a foreign tax credit, the terms of the credit are determined by the provisions, at the time a credit is given, of the U.S. statutory credit.

Therefore, the U.S. credit under the Convention is subject to the various limitations of U.S. law (see Code sections 901-908). For example, the credit against U.S. tax generally is limited to the amount of U.S. tax due with respect to net foreign source income within the relevant foreign tax credit limitation category (see Code section 904(a) and (d)), and the dollar amount of the credit is determined in accordance with U.S. currency translation rules (see, *e.g.*, Code section 986). Similarly, U.S. law applies to determine carryover periods for excess credits and other inter-year adjustments. When the alternative minimum tax is due, the alternative minimum tax foreign tax credit generally is limited in accordance with U.S. law to 90 percent of alternative minimum tax liability.

□□□*g*□□□□□□

Paragraph 2 provides a re-sourcing rule for gross income covered by paragraph 1. Paragraph 2 is intended to ensure that a U.S. resident can obtain a U.S. foreign tax credit for U.K. taxes paid when the Convention assigns to the United Kingdom primary taxing rights over an item of gross income. Although the U.S. Model does not contain a re-sourcing rule, the prior Convention does contain a similar rule.

Subparagraph (a) of paragraph 2 provides that, if the Convention allows the United Kingdom to tax an item of gross income (as defined under U.S. law) derived by a resident of the United States, the United States will treat that item of gross income as gross income from sources within the United Kingdom for U.S. foreign tax credit purposes. In the case of a U.S.-owned foreign corporation, however, section 904(g)(10) may apply for purposes of determining the U.S. foreign tax credit with respect to income subject to this re-sourcing rule. Section 904(g)(10) generally applies the foreign tax credit limitation separately to re-sourced income. Furthermore, the paragraph 2 re-sourcing rule applies to gross income, not net income. Accordingly, U.S. expense allocation and apportionment rules, see, *e.g.*, Treas. Reg. section 1.861-9, continue to apply to income resourced under paragraph 2.

According to the notes, if a U.S. resident receives a dividend described in subparagraph 1(b), it will be deemed to constitute income from sources within the United Kingdom, even if the dividend may be taxed only in the United States because the zero rate of withholding applies to it pursuant to paragraph 5 of Article 10 (Dividends).

Subparagraph (b) provides an exception to subparagraph (a) for gains derived by a U.S. resident from the sale of property governed by paragraph 6 of Article 13 (Gains). As discussed above in connection with Article 13 of the Convention, paragraph 6 generally preserves the taxing rights of the United Kingdom in cases of tax-motivated expatriation. Thus, under paragraph 6, if a U.K. resident gives up his U.K. residence by moving to a third country, sells property, and then re-establishes residence in the United Kingdom within five years, the United Kingdom may tax gains from the alienation of that property. The effect of subparagraph (b) of paragraph 2 of Article 24, however, is to ensure that the United States retains primary taxing rights over such gains if the former U.K. resident was a resident of the United States when he disposed of the property. Such gains are considered to be gains from sources within the United States. Accordingly, pursuant to paragraph 4 of Article 24, the United Kingdom would grant a credit for U.S. tax imposed upon such gains.

☐☐☐*g*☐☐☐☐☐☐

Paragraph 3 allows a limited U.S. foreign tax credit for the United Kingdom petroleum revenue tax. If the provisions of the Convention are relied upon to claim a foreign tax credit for the petroleum revenue tax, and any such tax would not otherwise be creditable under the Code, then the limitations of paragraph 3 apply, whether or not the tax is paid in the taxable year, and all of the petroleum revenue tax paid in the year must be treated as provided in the Convention. However, if a person chooses in a year not to rely upon the provisions of the Convention relevant to a claim for a foreign tax credit for the petroleum revenue tax, then the limitations provided by paragraph 3 would not apply in that year. Subject to the current overall foreign tax credit limitation of the Code, U.K. taxes creditable under the Code and creditable taxes paid in any other country can offset U.S. tax on income from U.K. and other foreign sources.

Under paragraph 1 of this article, the United States agrees to allow to its nationals and residents, as a direct or a deemed-paid credit against their U.S. tax, the appropriate amount of taxes paid or accrued to the United Kingdom by or on behalf of such nationals or residents on income separately assessed under the petroleum revenue tax. However, under paragraph 3, these foreign tax credits are limited to the amount attributable to income from sources within the United Kingdom.

The limitation prescribed by paragraph 3 is applied before the provisions and limitations relating to the foreign tax credit contained in the Code. These provisions include, among others, the rules in section 907 pertaining to foreign oil and gas extraction income and foreign oil related income. Application of the provisions of U.S. law as they now exist or as they may be amended from time to time (without changing the general principle of allowance of a credit) may limit the amount of petroleum revenue tax allowable as a credit in any taxable year to an amount less than that arrived at by applying the rules of paragraph 3.

Subparagraph (a) allows a U.S. foreign tax credit with respect to the petroleum revenue tax on extraction income from oil or gas wells in the United Kingdom, but the amount of the credit is limited to the product of the U.S. maximum corporate tax rate and the amount of the extraction income, minus the amount of any other U.K. tax on such income. The limit for a taxable year prescribed by subparagraph (a) of paragraph 3 is arrived at by making the computations explained in steps 1–4 below:

Step 1. The first step involves multiplying the maximum statutory U.S. tax rate applicable to the taxable income of a corporation for the taxpayer's taxable year by the amount of the taxpayer's taxable income (computed under U.S. standards) from the extraction of minerals from oil or gas wells in the United Kingdom.

The maximum statutory U.S. tax rate applicable to the taxable income of a corporation is the highest rate of tax specified in section 11 of the Code. This rate is currently 35 percent.

In arriving at taxable income from extraction for purposes of computing the limit, principles similar to those under section 907(c)(1) and (3) of the Code shall be applied. Taxable income from extraction includes taxable income derived by a person holding a royalty or other economic interest in an oil or gas well, even though the extraction is physically performed by a person other than the taxpayer.

Step 2. From the product arrived at under step 1 is subtracted other United Kingdom tax on income from the extraction of minerals from oil or gas wells in the United Kingdom. Because other United Kingdom tax may be calculated under United Kingdom law on a base which includes income from non-extraction activities, it may be necessary to allocate other United Kingdom tax to the income from extraction. In making this allocation, principles similar to those under section 907(c)(5) of the Code are to apply. The difference between the product computed under step 1 above and the other United Kingdom tax computed here is the limit with respect to the petroleum revenue tax on income from extraction.

Step 3. Under the relevant U.K. domestic law, it is possible for the petroleum revenue tax to be levied on what under U.S. standards would be income from activities other than extraction. Specifically, the base on which the petroleum revenue tax is computed is determined by reference to the value of oil or gas after initial transportation to the place in the United Kingdom (on land) at which the seller could reasonably be expected to deliver it, and after initial treatment and initial storage as defined under the U.K. law. Because of this, the total petroleum revenue tax paid or accrued must be allocated to income from extraction and to income from initial transportation, initial treatment, and initial storage.

The allocation of the petroleum revenue tax is to be made by multiplying the total petroleum revenue tax (other than amounts deemed to have been paid or accrued in the year by reason of the carry-back or carry-forward provisions set forth in subparagraphs (b) and (c) of paragraph 3) by a fraction, the numerator of which is taxable income from extraction (computed under U.S. standards, *i.e.*, the same number as that determined under step (1)) and the denominator of which is taxable income from extraction, initial transportation, initial treatment, and initial storage. If the denominator so computed is less than taxable income from extraction alone, then the denominator shall be taxable income from extraction.

Step 4. The lesser of the petroleum revenue tax paid or accrued with respect to extraction income under step 3 or the limit determined under Step 2 is treated as an income tax paid or accrued for the taxable year for purposes of computing the credit allowable under section 901. Such amount also is treated as oil and gas extraction taxes for purposes of section 907(c)(5) of the Code. Amounts in excess of the limit determined under Step 2 are not deductible if the taxpayer chooses to take to any extent the benefits of paragraph 1 of Article 24 for the taxable year.

Subparagraph (b) provides for a carryback and carryforward of the amount of the petroleum revenue tax disallowed by subparagraph (a). Where the petroleum revenue tax allocable to extraction income (determined under step 3 above) exceeds the credit limit provided under subparagraph (a) (determined under Step 2 above), such excess is treated as income tax paid or accrued in the second preceding taxable year, the first preceding taxable year, and in the first, second, third, fourth, or fifth succeeding taxable year, in that order and to the extent not deemed paid or accrued in a prior taxable year. In determining the year in which such petroleum revenue tax carried back or forward shall be deemed to have been paid, the limitation of subparagraph (a) of paragraph 3 shall apply.

If an amount of petroleum revenue tax which does not exceed the limit of subparagraph (a) is limited by application of sections 907 or 904 and is carried to another taxable year pursuant to sections 907 or 904, the amount treated as paid or accrued in such other taxable year will be treated as an income tax and will not be again subject to the limitation of paragraph 3.

Subparagraph (c) applies to determine the limit on the credit for the petroleum revenue tax with respect to income from initial transportation, initial treatment, and initial storage. These three items of income are to be combined for this purpose. The limit is computed by applying, ☐ ▯▯▯▯▯▯▯▯ ▯▯▯▯▯▯▯, steps 1, 2 and 4 described with respect to subparagraph (a) above. As with extraction, taxable income is to be determined by U.S. standards. The petroleum revenue tax allocable to initial transportation, treatment, and storage is the petroleum revenue tax paid or accrued in the current year not allocable to extraction income. The petroleum revenue tax allocated to initial transportation, initial treatment, and initial storage is not treated as oil and gas extraction tax under section 907(c)(5) of the Code but instead is treated as income tax on foreign oil related income within the meaning of section 907(c)(2) of the Code.

Where the petroleum revenue tax allocable to initial transportation, initial treatment, and initial storage exceeds the limit of subparagraph (c) for the taxable year, such excess shall be deemed paid or accrued under subparagraph (c) in the second preceding taxable year, the first preceding taxable year and in the first, second, third, fourth, or fifth succeeding taxable years, in that order and to the extent not deemed paid or accrued in a prior taxable year by reason of the limitation of subparagraph (c).

If an amount of petroleum revenue tax which does not exceed the limit of subparagraph (c) is limited by application of sections 907 or 904 and is carried to another taxable year pursuant to sections 907 or 904, the amount treated as paid or accrued in such other taxable year will be treated as an income tax and will not be again subject to the limitation of paragraph 3.

In the case of a U.S. company owning at least ten percent of the voting stock of a U.K. company from which the U.S. company receives dividends in any taxable year, the appropriate amount of petroleum revenue tax paid to the United Kingdom by that U.K. company with respect to the profits out of which such dividends are paid shall be a ratable portion of the petroleum revenue tax attributable to the accumulated profits out of which the dividend is paid.

Paragraph 4

The United Kingdom agrees, in paragraph 4, to allow to its citizens and residents a credit against U.K. tax for U.S. taxes. For this purpose, the U.S. taxes covered by clause (i) of subparagraph (a) of paragraph 3 and by paragraph 4 of Article 2 (Taxes Covered) are U.S. taxes.

Under subparagraph (a), the amount of U.S. tax payable under the laws of the United States and in accordance with this Convention, whether directly or by deduction, on profits, income or chargeable gains from sources within the United States (excluding, in the case of a dividend, United States tax in respect of the profits out of which the dividend is paid) is allowed as a credit against any United Kingdom tax computed by reference to the same profits, income or chargeable gains by reference to which the United States tax is computed.

Under subparagraph (b), in the case of a dividend paid by a company that is a resident of the United States to a company that is a resident of the United Kingdom and which controls directly or indirectly at least 10 percent of the voting power in the company paying the dividend, the credit takes into account (in addition to any U.S. tax for which credit may be allowed under the provisions of subparagraph (a) of this paragraph) the U.S. tax payable by the company in respect of the profits out of which such dividend is paid.

Subparagraph (c) eliminates the U.K. credit otherwise provided for in subparagraph (b) in certain circumstances. The rule is limited to certain cases where the two countries have a different view as to the ownership of dividends and, as a result, the United States has provided a tax deduction for payments that are measured by reference to the dividend. This rule is intended to apply to a particular type of financing transaction that has been widely used by U.K. resident companies to finance their U.S. operations. In this transaction, a U.S. holding company would sell stock in another U.S. company to a U.K. company. At the same time, it would enter into a repurchase agreement that would allow it to buy back the stock at a pre-determined price. The parties would structure the transactions in such a way that the sale and repurchase transactions would be treated as a loan for U.S. tax purposes. As a result, the dividends paid to the U.K. company are treated as payments of interest on the loan from the U.K. company to the U.S. company. The United Kingdom had seen a number of these transactions and was concerned about their potential impact.

U.K. law provides no mechanism by which to treat the sale and re-purchase in accordance with its economic substance. Accordingly, the United Kingdom is required by U.K.

domestic law to treat the U.K. company as the owner of the dividends for purposes of its rules, and to provide a foreign tax credit for the taxes paid by the U.S. company paying the dividends. However, recent changes to U.K. foreign tax credit rules allow the United Kingdom to deny credits if a tax treaty specifically so provides. The United Kingdom asked for the exception in paragraph (c) in order to conform the U.K. treatment of these transactions to the U.S. tax treatment. Because the rule applies only with respect to the indirect tax credit, it will apply only with respect to transactions involving persons who own more than 10 percent of the underlying company. Moreover, the rule applies only if the U.S. company receives an interest deduction that is based on the dividends paid with respect to the stock, while the deductible payments arising from standard sale-repurchase agreements would be based on a completely different measure, the current cost of funds. Accordingly, the rule should not (and is not intended to) affect most repos and similar transactions that take place in the public markets.

Subparagraph (c) would not be effective without subparagraph (d). Subparagraph (c) limits benefits that are otherwise available under domestic law and therefore would be inconsistent with the rules of paragraph 2 of Article 1 (General Scope), which provide that the tax treaty cannot limit benefits that are available under domestic law. Subparagraph (d) provides an exception from paragraph 2 of Article 1 with respect to subparagraph (c).

□□□□*g*□□□□□□

Paragraph 5 provides a re-sourcing rule for gross income covered by paragraph 4. This provision is intended to ensure that a U.K. resident can obtain a U.K. foreign tax credit for U.S. taxes paid when the Convention assigns to the United States primary taxing rights over an item of gross income. Paragraph 5 provides that, if the Convention allows the United States to tax an item of gross income (as defined under U.K. law) derived by a resident of the United Kingdom, the United Kingdom will treat that item of gross income as gross income from sources within the United States for U.K. foreign tax credit purposes. However, paragraph 6 of this article provides special rules where a U.S. citizen resident in the United Kingdom is subject to tax in the United States by reason of his citizenship under the saving clause of paragraph 4 of Article 1 (General Scope). According to the MOU, if a U.K. resident receives a dividend described in subparagraph (b) of paragraph 4, it will be deemed to constitute income from sources within the United States, even if the dividend may be taxed only in the United Kingdom because the zero rate of withholding applies to it.

□□□□*g*□□□□□□

Paragraph 6 provides special rules for the tax treatment in both States of certain types of income derived from U.S. sources by U.S. citizens who are resident in the United Kingdom. Since U.S. citizens, regardless of residence, are subject to United States tax at ordinary progressive rates on their worldwide income, the U.S. tax on the U.S. source income of a U.S. citizen resident in the United Kingdom may exceed the U.S. tax that may be imposed under the Convention on an item of U.S. source income derived by a resident of the United Kingdom who is not a U.S. citizen. This confirms that the United Kingdom retains primary taxing rights with respect to income derived by a resident that the United States may tax pursuant to section 877 of the Code.

Subparagraph (a) of paragraph 6 carries over a rule from the prior Convention which states that the United Kingdom is not bound to provide a credit for U.S. taxes with respect to income from sources outside the United States, as determined under U.K. law. Thus, for example, if a U.S. citizen resident in the United Kingdom derives income from sources within France, as determined under the source rules of the United Kingdom, then the United Kingdom is not required to give a credit for U.S. income tax imposed upon that income. In that case, the United States would give a credit for the tax paid to the United Kingdom, as well as any French taxes, with respect to such income. This rule ensures that, as between the State of residence and the State of citizenship, the State of residence takes priority.

Subparagraph (b) follows the U.S. Model by providing, with respect to items of income from sources within the United States, special credit rules for the United Kingdom. These rules apply to items of U.S.-source income that would be either exempt from U.S. tax or subject to reduced rates of U.S. tax under the provisions of the Convention if they had been received by a U.K. resident who is not a U.S. citizen. The U.K. tax credit allowed under paragraph 4 with respect to such items need not exceed the U.S. tax that may be imposed under the Convention, other than tax imposed solely by reason of the U.S. citizenship of the taxpayer under the provisions of the saving clause of paragraph 4 of Article 1 (General Scope).

For example, if a U.S. citizen resident in the United Kingdom receives portfolio dividends from sources within the United States, the foreign tax credit granted by the United Kingdom would be limited to 15 percent of the dividend -- the U.S. tax that may be imposed under subparagraph (b) of paragraph 2 of Article 10 (Dividends) -- even if the shareholder is subject to U.S. net income tax because of his U.S. citizenship. With respect to royalty or interest income, the United Kingdom would allow no foreign tax credit, because its residents are exempt from U.S. tax on these classes of income under the provisions of Articles 11 (Interest) and 12 (Royalties).

Paragraph 6(c) eliminates the potential for double taxation that can arise because subparagraph 6(b) provides that the United Kingdom need not provide full relief for the U.S. tax imposed on its citizens resident in the United Kingdom. The subparagraph provides that the United States will credit the income tax paid or accrued to the United Kingdom, after the application of subparagraph 6(b). It further provides that in allowing the credit, the United States will not reduce its tax below the amount that is taken into account in the United Kingdom in applying subparagraph 6(b).

Since the income described in paragraph 6(b) is U.S. source income, special rules are required to re-source some of the income to the United Kingdom in order for the United States to be able to credit the U.K. tax. This re-sourcing is provided for in subparagraph 6(d), which deems the items of income referred to in subparagraph 6(b) to be from foreign sources to the extent necessary to avoid double taxation under paragraph 6(c). In most cases, the income described in subparagraph 6(a) will be from sources outside the United States under U.S. rules, so it is not necessary for paragraph 6(d) to re-source the income in order to relieve double taxation. Subparagraph 3(e) of Article 26 (Mutual Agreement Procedure) provides a mechanism by which the competent authorities can resolve any disputes regarding whether income is from sources within the United States.

The following two examples illustrate the application of paragraph 6 in the case of a U.S.-source portfolio dividend received by a U.S. citizen resident in the United Kingdom. In both examples, the U.S. rate of tax on residents of the United Kingdom, under subparagraph (b) of paragraph 2 of Article 10 (Dividends) of the Convention, is 15 percent. In both examples, the U.S. income tax rate on the U.S. citizen is 36 percent. In example 1, the U.K. income tax rate on its resident (the U.S. citizen) is 25 percent (below the U.S. rate), and in example 2, the U.K. rate on its resident is 40 percent (above the U.S. rate).

	Example 1	Example 2
Subparagraph (b)		
U.S. dividend declared	$100.00	$100.00
Notional U.S. withholding tax (Article 10(2)(b))	15.00	15.00
U.K. taxable income	100.00	100.00
U.K. tax before credit	25.00	40.00
U.K. foreign tax credit	15.00	15.00
Net post-credit U.K. tax	10.00	25.00
Subparagraphs (c) and (d)		
U.S. pre-tax income	$100.00	$100.00
U.S. pre-credit citizenship tax	36.00	36.00
Notional U.S. withholding tax	15.00	15.00
U.S. tax available for credit	21.00	21.00
Income re-sourced from U.S. to U.K. (see below)	27.77	58.33
U.S. tax on re-sourced income	10.00	21.00
U.S. credit for U.K. tax	10.00	21.00
Net post-credit U.S. tax	11.00	0.00
Total U.S. tax	26.00	15.00

In both examples, in the application of subparagraph (b), the United Kingdom credits a 15 percent U.S. tax against its residence tax on the U.S. citizen. In the first example, the net U.K. tax after the U.K. foreign tax credit is $10.00; in the second example, it is $25.00. In the application of subparagraphs (c) and (d), from the U.S. tax due before credit of $36.00, the United States subtracts the amount of the U.S. source tax of $15.00, against which no U.S. foreign tax credit is allowed. This subtraction ensures that the United States collects the tax that it is due under the Convention as the State of source.

In both examples, given the 36 percent U.S. tax rate, the maximum amount of U.S. tax against which credit for the U.K. tax may be claimed is $21 ($36 U.S. tax minus $15 U.S. withholding tax). Initially, all of the income in both examples was from sources within the United States. For a U.S. foreign tax credit to be allowed for the full amount of the U.K. tax, an appropriate amount of the income must be re-sourced to the United Kingdom under subparagraph (d).

The amount that must be re-sourced depends on the amount of U.K. tax for which the U.S. citizen is claiming a U.S. foreign tax credit. In example 1, the U.K. tax was $10. For this amount to be creditable against U.S. tax, $27.77 ($10 U.K. tax divided by 36 percent U.S. tax rate) must be resourced to the United Kingdom. When the U.K. tax is credited against the U.S. tax on this resourced income, there is a net U.S. tax of $11 due after credit ($21 U.S. tax minus $10 U.K. tax). Thus, in example 1, there is a total of $26 in U.S. tax ($15 U.S. withholding tax plus $11 residual U.S. tax).

In example 2, the U.K. tax was $25, but, because the United States subtracts the U.S. withholding tax of $15 from the total U.S. tax of $36, only $21 of U.S. taxes may be offset by U.K. taxes. Accordingly, the amount that must be resourced to the United Kingdom is limited to the amount necessary to ensure a U.S. foreign tax credit for $21 of U.K. tax, or $58.33 ($21 U.K. tax divided by 36 percent U.S. tax rate). When the U.K. tax is credited against the U.S. tax on this re-sourced income, there is no residual U.S. tax ($21 U.S. tax minus $21 U.K. tax). Thus, in example 2, there is a total of $15 in U.S. tax ($15 U.S. withholding tax plus $0 residual U.S. tax). Although the U.K. tax was $25 and the U.S. tax available for credit was $21, there is no excess U.S. tax credit available for carryover.

Relationship to other articles

By virtue of subparagraph (a) of paragraph 5 of Article 1 (General Scope), Article 24 is not subject to the saving clause of paragraph 4 of Article 1. Thus, the United States will allow a credit to its citizens and residents in accordance with the Article, even if such credit were to provide a benefit not available under the Code (such as the re-sourcing provided by paragraph 2 and subparagraph 3(d)).

Article 25 (Non-Discrimination)

This Article assures that nationals of a Contracting State, in the case of paragraph 1, and residents of a Contracting State, in the case of paragraphs 2 through 4, will not be subject, directly or indirectly, to discriminatory taxation in the other Contracting State. For this purpose, non-discrimination means providing national treatment. Not all differences in tax treatment, either as between nationals of the two States, or between residents of the two States, are violations of this national treatment standard. Rather, the national treatment obligation of this Article applies only if the nationals or residents of the two States are comparably situated.

Each of the relevant paragraphs of the Article provides that two persons that are comparably situated must be treated similarly. Although the actual words differ from paragraph to paragraph (*e.g.*, paragraph 1 refers to two nationals "in the same circumstances," paragraph 2 refers to two enterprises "carrying on the same activities" and paragraph 4 refers to two enterprises that are "similar"), the common underlying premise is that if the difference in treatment is directly related to a tax-relevant difference in the situations of the domestic and foreign persons being compared, that difference is not to be treated as discriminatory (i.e., if one person is taxable in a Contracting State on worldwide income and the other is not, or tax may be collectible from one person at a later stage, but not from the other, distinctions in treatment would be justified under paragraph 1). Other examples of such factors that can lead to non-discriminatory differences in treatment are noted in the discussions of each paragraph.

The operative paragraphs of the Article also use different language to identify the kinds of differences in taxation treatment that will be considered discriminatory. For example, paragraphs 1 and 4 speak of "any taxation or any requirement connected therewith that is more burdensome," while paragraph 2 specifies that a tax "shall not be less favorably levied." Regardless of these differences in language, only differences in tax treatment that materially disadvantage the foreign person relative to the domestic person are properly the subject of the Article.

☐☐☐g☐☐☐☐☐☐

Paragraph 1 provides that a national of one Contracting State may not be subject to taxation or connected requirements in the other Contracting State that are more burdensome than the taxes and connected requirements imposed upon a national of that other State in the same circumstances. The OECD Model prohibits taxation that is "other than or more burdensome" than that imposed on U.S. persons. This Convention, consistent with the U.S. Model, omits the reference to taxation that is "other than" that imposed on U.S. persons because the only relevant question under this provision should be whether the requirement imposed on a national of the United Kingdom is more burdensome. A requirement may be different from the requirements imposed on U.S. nationals without being more burdensome.

As noted above, whether or not the two persons are both taxable on worldwide income is a significant circumstance for this purpose. The 1992 revision of the OECD Model added, after the words "in the same circumstances," the phrase "in particular with respect to residence," reflecting the fact that under most countries' laws residents are taxable on worldwide income and nonresidents are not. Since in the United States nonresident citizens are also taxable on worldwide income the Convention, like the U.S. Model, expands the phrase to refer, not to residence, but to taxation on worldwide income. Unlike the U.S. and OECD Models, however, the application of paragraph 1 does not extend to nationals of the Contracting States who are not residents of one of the Contracting States. The provision extending application to such nationals was excluded from the Convention at the request of the United Kingdom, consistent with their observation on Article 24 (Non-discrimination) of the OECD Model.

The term "national" in relation to a Contracting State is defined in subparagraph 1(h) of Article 3 (General Definitions). The term includes both individuals and juridical persons.

☐☐☐g☐☐☐☐☐

Paragraph 2 of the Article, like the comparable paragraphs in the OECD and U.S. Models, provides that a Contracting State may not tax a permanent establishment of an enterprise of the other Contracting State less favorably than an enterprise of that first-mentioned State that is carrying on the same activities.

The fact that a U.S. permanent establishment of an enterprise of the United Kingdom is subject to U.S. tax only on income that is attributable to the permanent establishment, while a U.S. corporation engaged in the same activities is taxable on its worldwide income is not, in itself, a sufficient difference to deny national treatment to the permanent establishment. There are cases, however, where the two enterprises would not be similarly situated and differences in treatment may be warranted. For instance, it would not be a violation of the non-discrimination protection of paragraph 2 to require the foreign enterprise to provide information in a reasonable manner that may be different from the information requirements imposed on a resident enterprise, because information may not be as readily available to the Internal Revenue Service from a foreign as from a domestic enterprise. Similarly, it would not be a violation of paragraph 2 to impose penalties on persons who fail to comply with such a requirement (see, *e.g.*, sections 874(a) and 882(c)(2)). Further, a determination that income and expenses have been attributed or allocated to a permanent establishment in conformity with the principles of Article 7 (Business Profits) implies that the attribution or allocation was not discriminatory.

Section 1446 of the Code imposes on any partnership with income that is effectively connected with a U.S. trade or business the obligation to withhold tax on amounts allocable to a foreign partner. In the context of the Convention, this obligation applies with respect to a share of the partnership income of a partner resident in the United Kingdom, and attributable to a U.S. permanent establishment. There is no similar obligation with respect to the distributive shares of U.S. resident partners. It is understood, however, that this distinction is not a form of discrimination within the meaning of paragraph 2 of the Article. No distinction is made between U.S. and non-U.S. partnerships, since the law requires that partnerships of both U.S. and non-U.S. domicile withhold tax in respect of the partnership shares of non-U.S. partners. Furthermore, in distinguishing between U.S. and non-U.S. partners, the requirement to withhold on the non-U.S. but not the U.S. partner's share is not discriminatory taxation, but, like other withholding on nonresident aliens, is merely a reasonable method for the collection of tax from persons who are not continually present in the United States, and as to whom it otherwise may be difficult for the United States to enforce its tax jurisdiction. If tax has been over-withheld, the partner can, as in other cases of over-withholding, file for a refund.

□□□□*g*□□□□□□

Paragraph 3 prohibits discrimination in the allowance of deductions. When a resident or an enterprise of a Contracting State pays interest, royalties or other disbursements to a resident of the other Contracting State, the first-mentioned Contracting State must allow a deduction for those payments in computing the taxable profits of the resident or enterprise as if the payment had been made under the same conditions to a resident of the first-mentioned Contracting State. Paragraph 3, however, does not require a Contracting State to give non-residents more favorable treatment than it gives to its own residents. Consequently, a Contracting State does not have to allow non-residents a deduction for items that are not deductible under its domestic law (for example, expenses of a capital nature).

The term "other disbursements" is understood to include a reasonable allocation of executive and general administrative expenses, research and development expenses and other expenses incurred for the benefit of a group of related persons that includes the person incurring the expense.

The opening part of the paragraph lists provisions of the Convention where the protection it gives for deductions does not apply. These are concerned with transactions involving potential abuse, where it is appropriate for the Contracting States to continue to apply their anti-avoidance safeguards. The paragraph carves out from its coverage not only the special relationship paragraphs at paragraph 4 of Article 11 (Interest), paragraph 4 of Article 12 (Royalties) and paragraph 3 of Article 22 (Other Income), but also the conduit arrangement test in paragraph 5 of Articles 7 (Business Profits), paragraph 9 of Article 10 (Dividends), paragraph 7 of Article 11, paragraph 5 of Article 12, and paragraph 4 of Article 22. Neither State is forced to apply the non-discrimination principle in such cases. The exception with respect to paragraph 4 of Article 11 would include the denial or deferral of certain interest deductions under Code section 163(j).

□□□□*g*□□□□□□

Paragraph 4 requires that a Contracting State not impose more burdensome taxation or connected requirements on an enterprise of that State that is wholly or partly owned or controlled, directly or indirectly, by one or more residents of the other Contracting State than the taxation or connected requirements that it imposes on other similar enterprises of that first-mentioned Contracting State. For this purpose it is understood that "similar" refers to similar activities or ownership of the enterprise.

This rule, like all non-discrimination provisions, does not prohibit differing treatment of entities that are in differing circumstances. Rather, a protected enterprise is only required to be treated in the same manner as other enterprises that, from the point of view of the application of the tax law, are in substantially similar circumstances both in law and in fact. The taxation of a distributing corporation under section 367(e) on an applicable distribution to foreign shareholders does not violate paragraph 4 of the Article because a foreign-owned corporation is not similar to a domestically-owned corporation that is accorded nonrecognition treatment under sections 337 and 355.

For the reasons given above in connection with the discussion of paragraph 2 of the Article, it is also understood that the provision in section 1446 of the Code for withholding of tax on non-U.S. partners does not violate paragraph 4 of the Article.

It is further understood that the ineligibility of a U.S. corporation with nonresident alien shareholders to make an election to be an "S" corporation does not violate paragraph 4 of the Article. If a corporation elects to be an S corporation (requiring 75 or fewer shareholders), it is generally not subject to income tax and the shareholders take into account their pro rata shares of the corporation's items of income, loss, deduction or credit. (The purpose of the provision is to allow an individual or small group of individuals to conduct business in corporate form while paying taxes at individual rates as if the business were conducted directly.) A nonresident alien does not pay U.S. tax on a net basis, and, thus, does not generally take into account items of loss, deduction or credit. Thus, the S corporation provisions do not exclude corporations with nonresident alien shareholders because such shareholders are foreign, but only because they are not net-basis taxpayers. Similarly, the provisions exclude corporations with other types of shareholders where the purpose of the provisions cannot be fulfilled or their mechanics implemented. For example, corporations with corporate shareholders are excluded because the purpose of the provision to permit individuals to conduct a business in corporate form at individual tax rates would not be furthered by their inclusion.

Paragraph 5 provides that a Contracting State is not obligated to grant to a resident of the other Contracting State any tax allowances, reliefs, etc., that it grants to its own residents on account of their civil status or family responsibilities. Thus, if a sole proprietor who is a resident of the United Kingdom has a permanent establishment in the United States, in assessing income tax on the profits attributable to the permanent establishment, the United States is not obligated to allow to the resident of the United Kingdom the personal allowances for himself and his family that he would be permitted to take if the permanent establishment were a sole proprietorship owned and operated by a U.S. resident, despite the fact that the individual income tax rates would apply.

Paragraph 6 of the Article confirms that no provision of the Article will prevent either Contracting State from imposing the branch profits tax described in paragraph 7 of Article 10 (Dividends).

As noted above, notwithstanding the specification in Article 2 (Taxes Covered) of taxes covered by the Convention for general purposes, for purposes of providing non-discrimination protection this Article applies to taxes of every kind and description imposed by a Contracting State or a political subdivision or local authority thereof. Customs duties are not considered to be taxes for this purpose.

The saving clause of paragraph 4 of Article 1 (General Scope) does not apply to this Article, by virtue of the exceptions in paragraph 5(a) of Article 1. Thus, for example, a U.S. citizen who is a resident of the United Kingdom may claim benefits in the United States under this Article.

Nationals of a Contracting State may claim the benefits of paragraph 1 regardless of whether they are entitled to benefits under Article 23 (Limitation on Benefits), because that paragraph applies to nationals and not residents. They may not claim the benefits of the other paragraphs of this Article with respect to an item of income unless they are generally entitled to treaty benefits with respect to that income under a provision of Article 23.

Article 26 (Mutual Agreement Procedure)

This article provides the mechanism for taxpayers to bring to the attention of the competent authorities of the Contracting States issues and problems that may arise under the Convention. This article also provides a mechanism for cooperation between the competent authorities of the Contracting States to resolve disputes and clarify issues that may arise under the Convention and to resolve cases of double taxation not provided for in the Convention. The competent authorities of the two Contracting States are identified in subparagraph (g) of paragraph 1 of Article 3 (General Definitions).

□□□□*g*□□□□□□

This paragraph provides that where a person considers that the actions of one or both Contracting States will result in taxation that is not in accordance with the Convention he may present his case to the competent authority of the Contracting State of which he is a resident or national.

Although the typical cases brought under this paragraph will involve economic double taxation arising from transfer pricing adjustments, the scope of this paragraph is not limited to such cases. For example, if the United States treats income derived by a company resident in the United Kingdom as attributable to a permanent establishment in the United States, and the U.K. resident believes that the income is not attributable to a permanent establishment, or that no permanent establishment exists, the U.K. company may bring a complaint under paragraph 1 to the competent authority of the United Kingdom.

It is not necessary for a person bringing a complaint first to have exhausted the remedies provided under the national laws of the Contracting States before presenting a case to the competent authorities. However, unlike the U.S. Model, but like the OECD Model, paragraph 1 provides that a case must be presented to a competent authority within a specified period. This period ends on the later of (1) the date three years from the first notification of the action giving rise to taxation not in accordance with the provisions of the Convention, or (2) the date six years from the end of the taxable year or chargeable period in respect of which that taxation is imposed or proposed. For example, if the taxpayer were notified by the United Kingdom on June 15, 2007 of a transfer pricing adjustment that affected the taxpayer's U.S. taxable year ended December 31, 2002, the taxpayer could present the case to the U.S. competent authority at any time before June 15, 2010. This would be true even though the date three years after first notification fell more than six years after the end of the taxpayer's taxable year. Alternatively, if the taxpayer were notified of the proposed adjustment on June 15, 2004, the taxpayer could present the case to the U.S. competent authority at any time before December 31, 2008, even though that date is more than three years after first notification.

Paragraph 18 of the Commentary to Article 25 of the OECD Model states that identifying the date of the first notification, as referred to in paragraph 1, should be done in the manner most favorable to the taxpayer. For example, if an action results from the tax authority following a published procedure, the first notification would not be the date of publication of the procedure, but rather the date on which the taxpayer was first notified of the decision to apply the procedure to him.

□□□g□□□□□□

Paragraph 2 instructs the competent authorities in dealing with cases brought by taxpayers under paragraph 1. Paragraph 2 provides that if the competent authority of the Contracting State to which the case is presented judges the case to have merit, and cannot reach a unilateral solution, it shall seek an agreement with the competent authority of the other Contracting State, pursuant to which taxation not in accordance with the Convention will be avoided. According to the notes, during the period that a proceeding under this article is pending, any assessment and collection procedures shall be suspended. Any tax payable after completion of the procedures shall be subject to any applicable interest and penalties for as long as it remains unpaid.

Any agreement is to be implemented even if such implementation otherwise would be barred by the statute of limitations or by some other procedural limitation, such as a closing agreement. Paragraph 2, however, does not prevent the application of domestic-law procedural limitations that give effect to the agreement (*e.g.*, a domestic-law requirement that the taxpayer file a return reflecting the agreement within one year of the date of the agreement).

Where the taxpayer has entered a closing agreement (or other written settlement) with the United States before bringing a case to the competent authorities, the U.S. competent authority will endeavor only to obtain a correlative adjustment from the United Kingdom. □ee□ Rev. Proc. 2002-52, 2002-31 I.R.B. 242, § 7.04. Because, as specified in paragraph 2 of Article 1 (General Scope), the Convention cannot operate to increase a taxpayer's liability, temporal or other procedural limitations can be overridden only for the purpose of making refunds and not to impose additional tax.

□□□g□□□□□□

Paragraph 3 authorizes the competent authorities to resolve difficulties or doubts that may arise as to the application or interpretation of the Convention. The paragraph includes a non-exhaustive list of examples of the kinds of matters about which the competent authorities may reach agreement. This list is purely illustrative; it does not grant any authority that is not implicitly present as a result of the introductory sentence of paragraph 3.

The competent authorities may, for example, agree to the same allocation of income, deductions, credits or allowances between an enterprise in one Contracting State and its permanent establishment in the other (subparagraph (a)) or between related persons (subparagraph (b)). These allocations are to be made in accordance with the arm's length principle underlying Article 7 (Business Profits) and Article 9 (Associated Enterprises). Agreements reached under these subparagraphs may include agreement on a methodology for determining an appropriate transfer price, common treatment of a taxpayer's cost sharing arrangement, or upon an acceptable range of results under that methodology. As stated in the notes, both competent authorities will publish any principle of general application established by an agreement between them.

As indicated in subparagraphs (c), (d), (e) and (f), the competent authorities also may agree to settle a variety of conflicting applications of the Convention. They may agree to characterize particular items of income in the same way (subparagraph (c)), to characterize entities in a particular way (subparagraph (d)), to apply the same source rules to particular items of income (subparagraph (e)), and to adopt a common meaning of a term (subparagraph f)). They also may agree as to the application of the provisions of domestic law regarding penalties, fines, and interest in a manner consistent with the purposes of the Convention (subparagraph (h)).

Subparagraph (g) makes clear that the competent authorities can agree whether the conditions have been met for application of the conduit arrangement test in paragraph 5 of Article 7 (Business Profits), paragraph 9 of Article 10 (Dividends), paragraph 7 of Article 11 (Interest), paragraph 5 of Article 12 (Royalties) and paragraph 4 of Article 22 (Other Income). Because application of the conduit arrangement test, as defined in subparagraph (n) of paragraph 1 of Article 3 (General Definitions), is specific to the facts of each case, an agreement of the competent authorities with respect to application of the conduit arrangement test necessarily will relate to the particular facts of a case. If the competent authorities become aware of a type of tax avoidance transaction entered into by several taxpayers, it is anticipated that each competent authority will respond to that type of transaction by means of domestic law and procedures (rather than through the issuance of a general agreement) in order to deny benefits in appropriate cases.

Since the list under paragraph 3 is not exhaustive, the competent authorities may reach agreement on issues not enumerated in paragraph 3 if necessary to avoid double taxation. For example, the competent authorities may seek agreement on a uniform set of standards for the use of exchange rates, or agree on consistent timing of gain recognition with respect to a transaction to the extent necessary to avoid double taxation. Agreements reached by the competent authorities under paragraph 3 need not conform to the internal law provisions of either Contracting State.

Finally, paragraph 3 authorizes the competent authorities to consult for the purpose of eliminating double taxation in cases not provided for in the Convention and to resolve any difficulties or doubts arising as to the interpretation or application of the Convention. This provision is intended to permit the competent authorities to implement the treaty in particular cases in a manner that is consistent with its expressed general purposes. It permits the competent authorities to deal with cases that are within the spirit of the provisions but that are not specifically covered. An example of such a case might be double taxation arising from a transfer pricing adjustment between two permanent establishments of a third-country resident, one in the United States and one in the United Kingdom. Since no resident of a Contracting State is involved in the case, the Convention does not apply, but the competent authorities nevertheless may use the authority of the Convention to prevent the double taxation of income.

Paragraph 4 provides that the competent authorities may communicate with each other for the purpose of reaching an agreement. This makes clear that the competent authorities of the two Contracting States may communicate without going through diplomatic channels. Such communication may be in various forms, including, where appropriate, through face-to-face meetings of the competent authorities or their representatives.

A case may be raised by a taxpayer under a treaty with respect to a year for which a treaty was in force after the treaty has been terminated. In such a case, the ability of the competent authorities to act is limited. They may not exchange confidential information, nor may they reach a solution that varies from that specified in their respective domestic laws.

A case also may be brought to a competent authority under a treaty that is in force, but with respect to a year prior to the entry into force of the treaty. The scope of the competent authorities to address such a case is not constrained by the fact that the treaty was not in force when the transactions at issue occurred, and the competent authorities have available to them the full range of remedies afforded under this article.

International tax cases may involve more than two taxing jurisdictions (*e.g.*, transactions among a parent corporation resident in country A and its subsidiaries resident in countries B and C). As long as there is a complete network of treaties among the three countries, it should be possible, under the full combination of bilateral authorities, for the competent authorities of the three States to work together on a three-sided solution. Although country A may not be able to give information received under Article 27 (Exchange of Information and Administrative Assistance) from country B to the authorities of country C, if the competent authorities of the three countries are working together, it should not be a problem for them to arrange for the authorities of country B to give the necessary information directly to the tax authorities of country C, as well as to those of country A. Each bilateral part of the trilateral solution must, of course, not exceed the scope of the authority of the competent authorities under the relevant bilateral treaty.

Article 26 is not subject to the saving clause of paragraph 4 of Article 1 (General Scope) by virtue of the exceptions in paragraph 5(a) of that Article. Thus, rules, definitions, procedures, etc. that are agreed upon by the competent authorities under this Article may be applied by the United States with respect to its citizens and residents even if they differ from the comparable Code provisions. Similarly, as indicated above, U.S. law may be overridden to provide refunds of tax to a U.S. citizen or resident under this Article.

A person may seek relief under Article 26 regardless of whether he is generally entitled to benefits under Article 23 (Limitation on Benefits). As in all other cases, the competent authority is vested with the discretion to decide whether the claim for relief is justified.

Article 27 (Exchange of Information and Administrative Assistance)

□□□□*g*□□□□□□

This article provides for the exchange of information between the competent authorities of the Contracting States. The information to be exchanged is that which is necessary to carry out the provisions of the Convention or the domestic laws of the United States or the United Kingdom concerning the taxes covered by the Convention. Like the OECD Model and earlier U.S. Models, but unlike the most recent U.S. Model, paragraph 1 refers to information that is "necessary" for carrying out the provisions of the Convention. This term consistently has been interpreted as being equivalent to the term "relevant," as used in the most recent U.S. Model, and does not require a requesting State to demonstrate that it would be disabled from enforcing its tax laws unless it obtained a particular item of information. Unlike the U.S. Model, the Convention provides that exchange of information is limited to taxes that are identified in Article 2 (Taxes Covered). United Kingdom legislation for implementation of its income tax treaties does not provide authority to exchange information with respect to other types of taxes.

Exchange of information with respect to each State's domestic law is authorized insofar as the taxation under domestic law is not contrary to the Convention. Thus, for example, information may be exchanged with respect to a covered tax, even if the transaction to which the information relates is a purely domestic transaction in the requesting State and, therefore, the exchange is not made to carry out the Convention. An example of such a case is provided in the OECD Commentary: a company resident in the United States and a company resident in the United Kingdom transact business between themselves through a third-country resident company. Neither Contracting State has a treaty with the third State. To enforce their internal laws with respect to transactions of their residents with the third-country company (since there is no relevant treaty in force), the Contracting States may exchange information regarding the prices that their residents paid in their transactions with the third-country resident.

Paragraph 1 clarifies that information may be exchanged that relates to the assessment or collection of, the enforcement or prosecution in respect of, or the determination of appeals in relation to, the taxes covered by the Convention. Thus, the competent authorities may request and provide information for cases under examination or criminal investigation, in collection, on appeals, or under prosecution.

Paragraph 1 states that information exchange is not restricted by Article 1 (General Scope). Accordingly, information may be requested and provided under this article with respect to persons who are not residents of either Contracting State. For example, if a third-country resident has a permanent establishment in the United Kingdom, which engages in transactions with a U.S. enterprise, the United States could request information with respect to that permanent establishment, even though the third-country resident is not a resident of either Contracting State. Similarly, if a third-country resident maintains a bank account in the United Kingdom, and the

Internal Revenue Service has reason to believe that funds in that account should have been reported for U.S. tax purposes but have not been so reported, information can be requested from the United Kingdom with respect to that person's account, even though that person is not the taxpayer under examination.

Paragraph 1 also provides assurances that any information exchanged will be treated as secret, subject to the same disclosure constraints as information obtained under the laws of the requesting State. Information received may be disclosed only to persons, including courts and administrative bodies, involved in the assessment, collection, or administration of, the enforcement or prosecution in respect of, or the determination of the of appeals in relation to, the taxes covered by the Convention. The information must be used by these persons in connection with the specified functions. Information may also be disclosed to legislative bodies, such as the tax-writing committees of Congress and the General Accounting Office, engaged in the oversight of the preceding activities. Information received by these bodies must be for use in the performance of their role in overseeing the administration of U.S. tax laws. Information received may be disclosed in public court proceedings or in judicial decisions.

The article authorizes the competent authorities to exchange information on a routine basis, on request in relation to a specific case, or spontaneously. It is contemplated that the Contracting States will utilize this authority to engage in all of these forms of information exchange, as appropriate.

□□□□*g*□□□□□□

Paragraph 2 provides that when information is requested by a Contracting State in accordance with this article, the other Contracting State is obligated to obtain the requested information as if the tax in question were the tax of the requested State, even if that State has no direct tax interest in the information requested. A change in the domestic law of the United Kingdom in 2000 allows the United Kingdom to agree to this provision by treaty.

□□□□*g*□□□□□□

Paragraph 3 provides that the obligations undertaken in paragraphs 1 and 2 to exchange information do not require a Contracting State to carry out administrative measures that are at variance with the laws or administrative practice of either State. Nor is a Contracting State required to supply information not obtainable under the laws or administrative practice of either State, or to disclose trade secrets or other information, the disclosure of which would be contrary to public policy. Thus, a requesting State may be denied information from the other State if the information would be obtained pursuant to procedures or measures that are broader than those available in the requesting State. However, each Contracting State has confirmed in the notes its ability to obtain and exchange certain information under Article 27. The information that may be exchanged includes information held by financial institutions, nominees, or persons acting in an agency or fiduciary capacity (but does not include information that would reveal confidential communications between a client and an attorney, solicitor or other legal representative, where the client seeks legal advice). In the case of the United States, the scope of the privilege for such confidential communications is coextensive with the attorney-client privilege under U.S. law.

The Contracting States may also obtain and exchange information relating to the ownership of legal persons.

As noted above, a change in U.K. domestic law in 2000 allows the United Kingdom to obtain and exchange information pursuant to a tax treaty even if it does not need the information for its own tax purposes. Therefore, paragraph 3 does not prevent the United Kingdom from providing information in the circumstances described in paragraph 2. Accordingly, the U.K. observation to paragraph 16 of the OECD Commentary to Article 26 is not relevant to the Convention.

While paragraph 3 states conditions under which a Contracting State is not obligated to comply with a request from the other Contracting State for information, the requested State is not precluded from providing such information, and may, at its discretion, do so subject to the limitations of its internal law.

□□□□*g*□□□□□□

Paragraph 4 provides that the requesting State may specify the form in which information is to be provided so that the information can be usable in the judicial proceedings of the requesting State. The requested State should provide the information in the form requested to the same extent that it can obtain information in that form under its own laws and administrative practices with respect to its own taxes. In this regard, unlike the U.S. Model, paragraph 4 does not authorize the use of depositions of witnesses to obtain information under this article. Under current U.K. law and practice, the U.K. Inland Revenue does not have the authority to take such depositions.

□□□□*g*□□□□□□

Paragraph 5 provides for assistance in collection of taxes to the extent necessary to ensure that treaty benefits are enjoyed only by persons entitled to those benefits under the terms of the Convention. Under paragraph 5, a Contracting State will endeavor to collect on behalf of the other State only those amounts necessary to ensure that any exemption or reduced rate of tax at source granted under the Convention by that other State is not enjoyed by persons not entitled to those benefits. For example, if the payer of a U.S.-source portfolio dividend receives a Form W-8BEN or other appropriate documentation from the payee, the withholding agent is permitted to withhold at the portfolio dividend rate of 15 percent. If, however, the addressee is merely acting as a nominee on behalf of a third-country resident, paragraph 5 would obligate the United Kingdom to take collection action against a person for the difference in applicable withholding rates in response to a specific request from the U.S. competent authority. This paragraph also makes clear that the Contracting State asked to collect the tax is not obligated, in the process of providing such assistance, to carry out administrative measures that are different from those used in the collection of its own taxes, or that would be contrary to its sovereignty, security or public policy.

Paragraph 6 requires the competent authority of a Contracting State to notify the competent authority of the other Contracting State before sending officials to that State to interview individuals and examine books and records with the consent of persons subject to examination.

Paragraph 7 states that the competent authorities of the Contracting States shall consult with each other for the purpose of cooperating and advising in respect of any action to be taken in implementing this article. Although not contained in the U.S. Model, this paragraph has been retained from the prior Convention because it has been useful in encouraging contacts between the competent authorities.

Once the Convention is in force, the competent authority may seek information under the Convention with respect to a year prior to the entry into force of the Convention. Even though the prior Convention was in effect during the years in which the transaction at issue occurred, the exchange of information provisions of the Convention apply. In that case, the competent authorities have available to them the full range of information exchange provisions afforded under this Article. The notes confirm this understanding with respect to the effective date of the Article.

A tax administration may also seek information with respect to a year for which a treaty was in force after the treaty has been terminated. In such a case the ability of the other tax administration to act is limited. The treaty no longer provides authority for the tax administrations to exchange confidential information. They may only exchange information pursuant to domestic law.

Article 28 (Diplomatic Agents and Consular Officers)

This Article confirms that any fiscal privileges to which diplomatic or consular officials are entitled under general provisions of international law or under special agreements will apply notwithstanding any provisions to the contrary in the Convention. The agreements referred to include any bilateral agreements, such as consular conventions, that affect the taxation of diplomats and consular officials and any multilateral agreements dealing with these issues, such as the Vienna Convention on Diplomatic Relations and the Vienna Convention on Consular Relations. The U.S. generally adheres to the latter because its terms are consistent with customary international law.

The Article does not independently provide any benefits to diplomatic agents and consular officers. Article 19 (Government Service) does so, as do Code section 893 and a number of bilateral and multilateral agreements. In the event that there is a conflict between the Convention and international law or such other treaties, under which the diplomatic agent or consular official is entitled to greater benefits under the latter, the latter laws or agreements shall have precedence. Conversely, if the Convention confers a greater benefit than another agreement, the affected person could claim the benefit of the tax treaty.

Pursuant to subparagraph 5(b) of Article 1, the saving clause of paragraph 4 of Article 1 (General Scope) does not apply to override any benefits of this Article available to an individual who is neither a citizen of the United States nor has immigrant status in the United States.

Article 29 (Entry into Force)

This Article contains the rules for bringing the Convention into force and giving effect to its provisions.

□□□*g*□□□□□

Paragraph 1 provides for the ratification of the Convention by both Contracting States according to their constitutional and statutory requirements. Instruments of ratification shall be exchanged as soon as possible.

In the United States, the process leading to ratification and entry into force is as follows: Once a treaty has been signed by authorized representatives of the two Contracting States, the Department of State sends the treaty to the President who formally transmits it to the Senate for its advice and consent to ratification, which requires approval by two-thirds of the Senators present and voting. Prior to this vote, however, it generally has been the practice for the Senate Committee on Foreign Relations to hold hearings on the treaty and make a recommendation regarding its approval to the full Senate. Both Government and private sector witnesses may testify at these hearings. After receiving the Senate's advice and consent to ratification, the treaty is returned to the President for his signature on the ratification document. The President's signature on the document completes the process in the United States.

□□□*g*□□□□□

Paragraph 2 provides that the Convention will enter into force upon the exchange of instruments of ratification. The date on which a treaty enters into force is not necessarily the date on which its provisions take effect. Paragraph 2, therefore, also contains rules that determine when the provisions of the treaty will have effect. Under paragraph 2(a), the Convention will have effect with respect to taxes withheld at source (principally dividends, interest and royalties) for amounts paid or credited on or after the first day of the second month following the date on which the Convention enters into force. For example, if instruments of ratification are exchanged on April 25 of a given year, the withholding rates specified in paragraph 2 and 3 of Article 10 (Dividends) would be applicable to any dividends paid or credited on or after June 1 of that year. This rule allows the benefits of the withholding reductions to be put into effect as soon as possible, without waiting until the following year. The delay of one to two months is required to allow sufficient time for withholding agents to be informed about the change in withholding rates. If for some reason a withholding agent withholds at a higher rate than that provided by the Convention (perhaps because it was not able to re-program its computers before the payment is made), a beneficial owner of the income that is a resident of the United Kingdom may make a claim for refund pursuant to section 1464 of the Code.

With respect to other taxes (including the excise tax on insurance premiums and the branch profits tax), paragraph 2 specifies different effective dates for the United States and the United Kingdom. The differences reflect the differences between the tax and accounting periods in each Contracting State. With respect to the United States, the Convention will have effect with respect to taxes other than those withheld at source for any taxable period beginning on or after January 1 of the year following entry into force. With respect to the United Kingdom, there are different effective dates for different taxes. For all income taxes other than those withheld at source and capital gains taxes the Convention will have effect for any year of assessment beginning on or after April 6 next following the date on which the Convention enters into force. The Convention will have effect with respect to corporation taxes for any financial year beginning on or after April 1 next following the date on which the Convention enters into force. Finally, the Convention will have effect with respect to the U.K. petroleum revenue tax for chargeable periods beginning on or after January 1 of the year following entry into force.

As discussed under Articles 26 (Mutual Agreement Procedure) and 27 (Exchange of Information and Administrative Assistance), the notes confirm that the powers afforded the competent authority under these articles apply with respect to taxable periods preceding entry into force.

☐☐☐g☐☐☐☐☐☐

Paragraph 3 provides that the prior Convention generally ceases to have effect with respect to any tax as of the date this Convention takes effect with respect to that tax under paragraph 2. As in many recent U.S. treaties, however, paragraph 3 also provides an exception to this general rule. Under paragraph 3, if the prior Convention would have afforded greater relief from tax than this Convention, the prior Convention shall, at the election of any person that was entitled to benefits under the prior Convention, continue to have effect in its entirety for a twelve-month period from the date on which this Convention otherwise would have had effect with respect to such person.

Thus, a taxpayer may elect to extend the benefits of the prior Convention for one year from the date on which the relevant provision of the new Convention would first take effect. During the period in which the election is in effect, the provisions of the prior Convention will continue to apply only insofar as they applied before the entry into force of the Convention. If the grace period is elected, all of the provisions of the prior Convention must be applied for that additional year. The taxpayer may not apply certain, more favorable provisions of the prior Convention and, at the same time, apply other, more favorable provisions of this Convention. The taxpayer must choose one regime or the other.

For example, suppose the instruments of ratification are exchanged on April 1, 2003 and the Convention thus enters into force on that date. The new Convention would take effect with respect to taxes withheld at source for amounts paid or credited on or after June 1, 2003. If the election is made, the provisions of the prior Convention regarding withholding (including the rules of Article 16 (Investment or Holding Companies)) would continue to have effect for amounts paid or credited at any time prior to June 1, 2004. The provisions of the Convention regarding withholding (including the rules of Article 23 (Limitation on Benefits)) would have effect for amounts paid or credited on or after June 1, 2004. With respect to other U.S. taxes, the Convention would be applicable for fiscal periods beginning on or after January 1, 2004, unless the taxpayer made an election to allow the prior Convention to continue. If such an election is made, the Convention would be applicable for fiscal periods beginning on or after January 1, 2005.

The prior Convention shall terminate on the last date on which it has effect with respect to any tax in accordance with the provisions of paragraphs 3 and 4 of Article 29.

□□□*g*□□□□□□

Paragraph 4 provides an exception to the entry into force of this Convention and the termination of the prior Convention. The treatment of trainees under Article 21 (Students and Trainees) of the prior Convention may be more generous than the treatment of trainees under Article 20 (Students) of the Convention. Certain trainees may have based their decisions to come to the host State for training upon the assumption that Article 21 of the prior Convention would apply to them. Paragraph 5 ensures that the rules do not change with respect to such individuals. It provides that an individual who is entitled to the benefits of Article 21 of the prior Convention at the time of entry into force of this Convention shall continue to be entitled to such benefits as if the prior Convention had remained in force. This additional grandfather rule is necessary because there are circumstances in which the twelve-month grace period of paragraph 3 would not cover the entire period at issue.

Article 30 (Termination)

The Convention is to remain in effect indefinitely, unless terminated by one of the Contracting States in accordance with the provisions of Article 30. The Convention may be terminated at any time after the year in which the Convention enters into force. If notice of termination is given, the provisions of the Convention with respect to withholding at source will cease to have effect after the expiration of a period of 6 months beginning with the delivery of notice of termination. With respect to other taxes, the effective date of termination mirrors the rules with respect to entry into force. That is, the Convention will cease to have effect in the United States for taxable periods beginning on or after the date that is six months after the date on which notice of termination was given. For all income taxes other than those withheld at source and for capital gains taxes imposed by the United Kingdom, the Convention will cease to have effect for any year of assessment beginning on or after the date that is six months after the date on which notice of termination was given. The Convention will cease to have effect with respect to U.K. corporation taxes for any financial year beginning on or after the date that is six months after the date on which notice of termination was given. Finally, the Convention will cease to have effect with respect to the U.K. petroleum revenue tax for chargeable periods beginning on or after the date that is six months after the date on which notice of termination was given.

Article 30 relates only to unilateral termination of the Convention by a Contracting State. Nothing in that Article should be construed as preventing the Contracting States from concluding a new bilateral agreement, subject to ratification, that supersedes, amends or terminates provisions of the Convention without the six-month notification period.

Customary international law observed by the United States and other countries, as reflected in the Vienna Convention on Treaties, allows termination by one Contracting State at any time in the event of a "material breach" of the agreement by the other Contracting State.

DEPARTMENT OF THE TREASURY
WASHINGTON, D.C. 20220

July 19, 2002

Gabriel Makhlouf
Director
Inland Revenue, International
Victory House
30-34 Kingsway
London WC2B
United Kingdom

Dear Mr. Makhlouf:

As we have discussed, questions have been raised about the manner in which our respective tax examiners will administer the rules in our proposed income tax convention dealing with "conduit arrangements". We hope that an exchange of letters will provide useful guidance regarding the position in each country.

With respect to the United States, we intend to interpret the conduit arrangement provisions of the Convention in accordance with U.S. domestic law as it may evolve over time. The relevant law currently includes in particular the rules of regulation section 1.881-3 and other regulations adopted under the authority of section 7701(l) of the Internal Revenue Code. Therefore, the inclusion of the conduit arrangement rules in the Convention does not constitute an expansion (or contraction) of U.S. domestic anti-abuse principles (except with respect to the application of anti-conduit principles to the insurance excise tax).

We understand that the United Kingdom does not have domestic law provisions relating to conduit transactions. It has, however, entered into a number of treaties which include provisions aimed at dealing with conduit-type arrangements. We understand that the United Kingdom will, subject to the limitations in Article 3(1)(n), interpret the provisions in the proposed convention in a manner consistent with its practice under those other treaties.

In practice, of course, such general principles and practice will be applied to particular fact patterns in determining whether the anti-conduit provisions will apply. In order to further develop our mutual understanding of how we each propose to apply the language, I have set out below a number of examples together with the U.S. view regarding whether benefits would be denied in each case.

We would appreciate your views, including the reasoning behind your conclusion, regarding the treatment that would apply to each of the cases set out below if the situation were reversed and the United Kingdom were the source of the payments.

I look forward to your response regarding the U.K. views of these transactions (as reversed). I appreciate the opportunity for our teams to work together on this important matter.

Very truly yours,

Barbara M. Angus
International Tax Counsel

Example 1. UKCo, a publicly traded company organized in the United Kingdom, owns all of the outstanding stock of USCo. XCo, a company organized in a country that does not have a tax treaty with the United States, would like to purchase a minority interest in USCo, but believes that the 30% U.S. domestic withholding tax on dividends would make the investment uneconomic. UKCo proposes that USCo instead issue preferred stock to UKCo, paying a fixed return of 4% plus a contingent return of 20% of USCo's net profits. The maturity of the preferred stock is 20 years. XCo will enter into a separate contract with UKCo pursuant to which it pays to UKCo an amount equal to the issue price of the preferred stock and will receive from UKCo after 20 years the redemption price of the stock. During the 20 years, UKCo will pay to XCo 3 ¾% plus 20% of USCo's net profits.

This arrangement constitutes a conduit arrangement because UKCo participated in the transaction in order to achieve a reduction in U.S. withholding tax for XCo.

Example 2. USCo has issued only one class of stock, common stock that is 100% owned by UKCo, a company organized in the United Kingdom. UKCo also has only one class of common stock outstanding, all of which is owned by XCo, a company organized in a country that does not have a tax treaty with the United States. UKCo is engaged in the manufacture of electronics products, and USCo serves as UKCo's exclusive distributor in the United States. Under paragraph 4 of Article 23 (Limitation on Benefits), UKCo will be entitled to benefits with respect to dividends received from USCo, even though UKCo is owned by a resident of a third country.

Because the common stock owned by UKCo and XCo does not represent a "financing transaction" within the meaning of regulation section 1.881-3 as currently in effect, on these facts, this will not constitute a conduit arrangement.

Example 3. XCo, a company organized in a country that does not have a tax treaty with the United States, loans $1,000,000 to USCo, its wholly-owned U.S. subsidiary in exchange for a note issued by USCo. XCo later realizes that it can avoid the U.S. withholding tax by assigning the note to its wholly-owned subsidiary, UKCo. Accordingly, XCo assigns the note to UKCo in exchange for a note issued by UKCo. The USCo note pays 7% and the UKCo note pays 6 ¾%.

The transaction constitutes a conduit arrangement because it was structured to eliminate the U.S. withholding tax that XCo otherwise would have paid.

Example 4. XCo, a company organized in Country X, which does not have a tax treaty with the United States, owns all of the stock of USCo, a company resident in the United States. XCo has for a long time done all of its banking with UKCo, a company organized in the United Kingdom, because the banking system in Country X is relatively unsophisticated. As a result, XCo tends to maintain a large deposit with UKCo. UKCo is unrelated to XCo and USCo. When USCo needs a loan to fund an acquisition, XCo suggests that USCo deal with UKCo, which is already familiar with the business conducted by XCo and USCo. USCo discusses the loan with several different banks, all on terms similar to those offered by UKCo, but eventually enters into the loan with UKCo, in part because interest paid to UKCo would not be subject to U.S. withholding tax, while interest paid to banks organized in Country X would be.

The United States will consider the fact that UKCo is unrelated to USCo and XCo in determining whether there is a conduit arrangement. Accordingly, this will be treated as a conduit arrangement only if UKCo would not have entered into the transaction on substantially the same terms in the absence of the XCo deposit. Under these facts, there is no conduit arrangement.

Example 5. UKCo, a publicly-traded company organized in the United Kingdom, is the holding company for a manufacturing group in a highly competitive technological field. The manufacturing group conducts research in subsidiaries located around the world. Any patents developed in a subsidiary are licensed by the subsidiary to UKCo, which then licenses the technology to its subsidiaries that need it. UKCo keeps only a small spread with respect to the royalties it receives, so that most of the profit goes to the subsidiary that incurred the risk with respect to developing the technology. XCo, a company located in a country with which the United States does not have a tax treaty, has developed a process that will substantially increase the profitability of all of UKCo's subsidiaries, including USCo, a company organized in the United States. According to its usual practice, UKCo licenses the technology and sub-licenses the technology to its subsidiaries. USCo pays a royalty to UKCo, substantially all of which is paid to XCo.

Because UKCo entered into these transactions in the ordinary course of its business, and there is no indication that it established its licensing business in order to reduce its U.S. withholding tax, the arrangements among USCo, UKCo and XCo do not constitute a conduit arrangement.

Example 6. XCo is a publicly traded company resident in Country X, which does not have a tax treaty with the United States. XCo is the parent of a worldwide group of companies, including UKCo, a company resident in the United Kingdom, and USCo, a company resident in the United States. USCo is engaged in the active conduct of a trade or business in the United States. UKCo is responsible for coordinating the financing of all of the subsidiaries of XCo. UKCo maintains a centralized cash management accounting system for XCo and its subsidiaries in which it records all intercompany payables and receivables. UKCo is responsible for disbursing or receiving any cash payments required by transactions between its affiliates and unrelated parties. UKCo enters into interest rate and foreign exchange contracts as necessary to manage the risks arising from mismatches in incoming and outgoing cash flows. The activities of UKCo are intended (and reasonably can be expected) to reduce transaction costs and overhead and other fixed costs. UKCo has 50 employees, including clerical and other back office personnel, located in the United Kingdom.

XCo lends to UKCo DM 15 million (worth $10 million) in exchange for a 10-year note that pays interest annually at a rate of 5% per annum. On the same day, UKCo lends $10 million to USCo in exchange for a 10-year note that pays interest annually at a rate of 8% per annum. UKCo does not enter into a long-term hedging transaction with respect to these financing transactions, but manages the interest rate and currency risk arising from the transactions on a daily, weekly or quarterly basis by entering into forward currency contracts.

Because UKCo performs significant activities with respect to the transactions between USCo and XCo, the participation of UKCo is presumed not to have as one of its main purposes the avoidance of U.S. withholding tax. Accordingly, based upon the foregoing facts, the loan from XCo to UKCo and the loan from UKCo to USCo do not constitute a conduit arrangement under the Convention.

Inland
Revenue
International Division

Gabriel Makhlouf
Director

Victory House
30-34 Kingsway
London WC2B 6ES

Telephone: 020 7438 6762
International: +44 20 7438 6762
Fax: 020 7438 6396
International: +44 20 7438 6396
E-mail: gabs.makhlouf@ir.gsi.gov.uk

19 July 2002

Ms Barbara M Angus
International Tax Counsel
US Department of the Treasury
1500 Pennsylvania Avenue, NW
Washington, DC 20220

Dear Barbara,

Thank you for your letter of 19 July. I am happy to confirm that your understanding of the UK's position with regard to the application of the rules in our proposed income tax treaty dealing with "conduit arrangements" is correct.

I attach the examples, reversed to show the position where income flows from the UK to the US, together with our views on how we would apply the anti-conduit rules to the transactions described.

Yours,

G MAKHLOUF

Example 1

USCo, a publicly traded company organised in the United States, owns all of the outstanding stock of UKCo. XCo, a company organised in a country that does not have a tax treaty with the United Kingdom, would like to purchase a minority interest in UKCo. USCo proposes that UKCo issue preferred stock to USCo, paying a fixed return of 4% plus a contingent return of 20% of UKCo's net profits. The maturity of the preferred stock is 20 years. XCo will enter into a separate contract with USCo pursuant to which it pays to USCo an amount equal to the issue price of the preferred stock and will receive from USCo after 20 years the redemption price of the stock. During the 20 years, USCo will pay to XCo 3 ¾% plus 20% of UKCo's net profits.

The U.K. considers this arrangement would meet the objective definition of a conduit arrangement at Article 3(1)(n)(i) but because the U.K. has no withholding tax on dividends the motive test at Article 3(1)(n)(ii) would not be met because no increased treaty benefit would be obtained by the routing through the U.S. Therefore the arrangement would not constitute a conduit arrangement as defined by the treaty.

Example 2

UKCo has issued only one class of stock, common stock that is 100% owned by USCo, a company organized in the United States. USCo also has only one class of common stock outstanding, all of which is owned by XCo, a company organized in a country that does not have a tax treaty with the United Kingdom. USCo is engaged in the manufacture of electronics products, and UKCo serves as USCo's exclusive distributor in the United Kingdom. Under paragraph 4 of Article 23 (Limitation on Benefits), USCo will be entitled to benefits with respect to dividends received from UKCo, even though USCo is owned by a resident of a third country.

This seems to be a perfectly acceptable and normal commercial structure with real economic activity in both the U.S. and the U.K. The payment of dividends by subsidiary companies is a normal feature of commercial life. Accordingly, in the absence of evidence that dividends were flowed through to XCo, these transactions would not constitute a conduit arrangement.

Example 3

XCo, a company organized in a country that does not have a tax treaty with the United Kingdom, loans $1,000,000 to UKCo, its wholly-owned U.K. subsidiary in exchange for a note issued by UKCo. XCo later realizes that it can avoid the U.K. withholding tax by assigning the note to its wholly-owned subsidiary, USCo. Accordingly, XCo assigns the note to USCo in exchange for a note issued by USCo. The UKCo note pays 7% and the USCo note pays 6 ¾%.

The loan note was assigned to avoid U.K. income tax on the payment of interest. The transaction constitutes a conduit arrangement as defined in the treaty as both the objective definition and the motive test at Article 3(1)(n)(i) and (ii) respectively are met.

Example 4

XCo, a company organized in Country X, which does not have a tax treaty with the United Kingdom, owns all of the stock of UKCo, a company resident in the United Kingdom. XCo has for a long time done all of its banking with USCo, a company organized in the United States, because the banking system in Country X is relatively unsophisticated. As a result, XCo tends to maintain a large deposit with USCo. USCo is unrelated to XCo and UKCo. When UKCo needs a loan to fund an acquisition, XCo suggests that UKCo deal with USCo, which is already familiar with the business conducted by XCo and UKCo. UKCo discusses the loan with several different banks, all on terms similar to those offered by USCo, but eventually enters into the loan with USCo, in part because interest paid to USCo would not be subject to U.K. withholding tax, while interest paid to banks organized in Country X would be.

The fact that UK/US treaty benefits are available if UKCo borrows from USCo, and that similar benefits might not be available if it borrowed elsewhere, is clearly a factor in UKCo's decision (which may be influenced by advice given to it by its 100% shareholder). It may even be a decisive factor, in the sense that, all else being equal, the availability of treaty benefits may swing the balance in favour of borrowing from USCo rather than from another lender. However, whether the obtaining of treaty benefits was "the main purpose or one of the main purposes" of the transaction would have to be determined by reference to the particular facts and circumstances.

Similarly, for the anti-conduit provision to apply it would have to be established that the interest paid by UKCo was "flowing through" USCo to XCo. The fact that XCo has historically maintained large deposits with USCo might, if anything, be a counter-indication. Against that, there is the question why a cash-rich company would want to increase its overall debt exposure in this way. XCo could redirect its balance with USCo and lend it to UKCo – in which case it would face U.K. withholding tax. It chooses not to, so there is a possible argument that the transactions were structured to avoid U.K. withholding tax by obtaining benefits under the treaty.

On the specific facts as presented, the transactions would not constitute a conduit arrangement as defined by the treaty.

However, if USCo's decision to lend to UKCo was dependent on XCo providing a matching collateral deposit to secure the loan, the indication would be that XCo was in substance lending to UKCo direct but in form routing the loan through a bank with whom it has a close relationship in order to obtain the benefit of the treaty. In such circumstances the transactions would constitute a conduit arrangement as defined by the treaty.

Example 5

USCo, a publicly-traded company organized in the United States, is the holding company for a manufacturing group in a highly competitive technological field. The manufacturing group conducts research in subsidiaries located around the world. Any patents developed in a subsidiary are licensed by the subsidiary to USCo, which then licenses the technology to its subsidiaries that need it. USCo keeps only a small spread with respect to the royalties it receives, so that most of the profit goes to the subsidiary that incurred the risk with respect to developing the technology. XCo, a company located in a country with which the United Kingdom does not have a tax treaty, has developed a process that will substantially increase the profitability of all of USCo's subsidiaries, including UKCo, a company organized in the United Kingdom. According to its usual practice, USCo licenses the technology and sub-licenses the technology to its subsidiaries. UKCo pays a royalty to USCo, substantially all of which is paid to XCo.

Because XCo is conforming to the standard commercial organisation and behaviour of the group in the way that it structures its licensing and sub-licensing activities and assuming the same structure is employed with respect to other subsidiaries carrying out similar activities in countries which have treaties which offer similar or more favourable benefits, the inference would be that the absence of a treaty between country X and the UK is not influencing the motive for the transactions described.

Therefore even though the specific fact pattern, as presented, meets the first part of the definition of a "conduit arrangement" at Article 3(1)(n)(i), on balance the conclusion would be that "the main purpose or one of the main purposes" of the transactions was not the obtaining of UK/US treaty benefits. So the structure would not constitute a conduit arrangement.

Example 6

XCo is a publicly traded company resident in Country X, which does not have a tax treaty with the United Kingdom. XCo is the parent of a worldwide group of companies, including USCo, a company resident in the United States, and UKCo, a company resident in the United Kingdom. UKCo is engaged in the active conduct of a trade or business in the United Kingdom. USCo is responsible for coordinating the financing of all of the subsidiaries of XCo. USCo maintains a centralized cash management accounting system for XCo and its subsidiaries in which it records all inter-company payables and receivables. USCo is responsible for disbursing or receiving any cash payments required by transactions between its affiliates and unrelated parties. USCo enters into interest rate and foreign exchange contracts as necessary to manage the risks arising from mismatches in incoming and outgoing cash flows. The activities of USCo are intended (and reasonably can be expected) to reduce transaction costs and overhead and other fixed costs. USCo has 50 employees, including clerical and other back office personnel, located in the United States.

XCo lends to USCo DM 15 million (worth $10 million) in exchange for a 10-year note that pays interest annually at a rate of 5% per annum. On the same day, USCo lends $10 million to UKCo in exchange for a 10-year note that pays interest annually at a rate of 8% per annum. USCo does not enter into a long-term hedging transaction with respect to these financing transactions, but manages the interest rate and currency risk arising from the transactions on a daily, weekly or quarterly basis by entering into forward currency contracts.

UKCo appears to be a real business performing substantive economic functions, using real assets and assuming real risks. USCo appears to be bearing the interest rate and currency risk. It is assumed that the transactions are typical of USCo's normal treasury business and that that business was carried on in a commercial manner.

So, on the specific facts presented, the transactions would not constitute a conduit arrangement as defined by the treaty.